Socktopus

Socktopus

17 pairs of socks
to knit and show off

Alice Yu

The Taunton Press

The Taunton Press, Inc., 63 South Main Street, PO Box 5506, Newtown, CT 06470-5506
email: tp@taunton.com

First published 2011 by Guild of Master Craftsman Publications Ltd
Castle Place, 166 High Street, Lewes, East Sussex BN7 1XU

Library of Congress Cataloging-in-Publication Data

Yu, Alice.
  Socktopus : 17 pairs of socks to knit and show off / Alice Yu.
      p. cm.
  ISBN 978-1-60085-410-1 (pbk.)
  1. Knitting--Patterns. 2. Socks. I. Title.
  TT825.Y8 2011
  746.43'2--dc23

                        2011019763

Publisher Jonathan Bailey
Production Manager Jim Bulley
Managing Editor Gerrie Purcell
Project Editor Judith Chamberlain-Webber
Editor Judith Durant
Managing Art Editor Gilda Pacitti
Photographer Chris Gloag
Designer Simon Goggin

Set in American Typewriter and Interstate
Color origination by GMC Reprographics
Printed and bound by Hung Hing Printing Co. Ltd. in China
10 9 8 7 6 5 4 3 2 1

Contents

PATTERN GALLERY

Totally Vanilla 32

Kandahar 38

V Junkie 46

2luvcrew 76

Vorticity 84

Rumpled! 90

Hundred Acre Wood 116

De Stijl 124

Fiori di Zucca 130

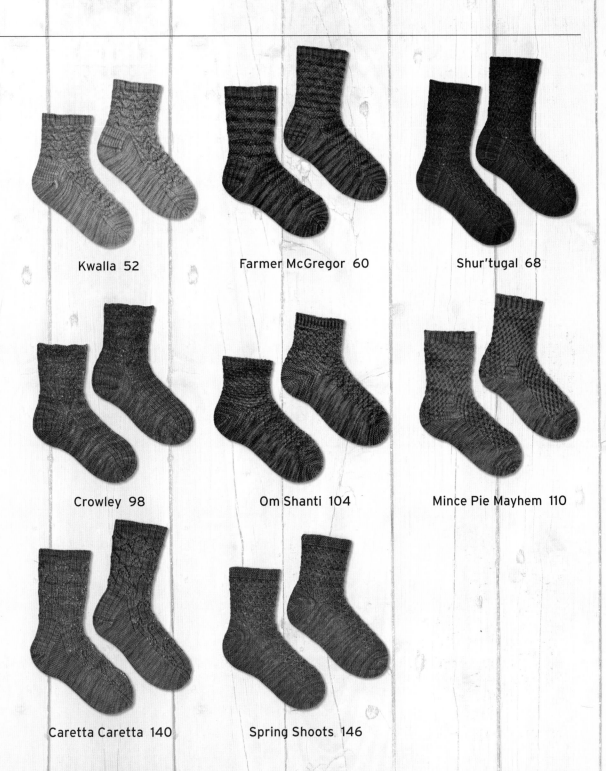

Kwalla 52

Farmer McGregor 60

Shur'tugal 68

Crowley 98

Om Shanti 104

Mince Pie Mayhem 110

Caretta Caretta 140

Spring Shoots 146

Introduction

Socks are my addiction. I admit it. I have no problem saying, "I am a Sock Addict." I love knitting them. I love wearing them—feet swaddled in little clouds is how I would describe the feeling. The yarns, the fibers, the designs; wearing them, gifting them, receiving them. Oh the joy a beautifully knitted pair of socks can bring! There are so many reasons why hand knit socks simply rock; here are my top 10.

1 Good things come in small packages

A pair of socks will fit in the palm of your hand. You can keep a pair in your pocket (some people have cold floors, you know), or tuck them in your purse. Need a surprise present? Nothing says surprise like pulling a pair of (hopefully new and unworn) hand knit socks from your back pocket. Can't do that with a waffle iron, can you?

2 Socks are commitment-phobe friendly

New to knitting? Want to make something but don't want to spend weeks/months/years/decades (delete as appropriate) knitting it? Don't want to spend a fortune on 20 skeins of yarn only to find you've knit two skeins worth in two years? A single sock can be knit in about 10 hours with less than 50 grams of yarn. No need for any big commitments.

3 Socks encourage promiscuity

While being perfect for the commitment-phobe, socks are also great projects for the WIP (work-in-progress) tarts out there. Like peacocks strutting their stuff, sock yarns entice and mesmerize with their brilliant hues and infinite variety of colors. They are designed to lure us away from current WIPs and bewitch us into casting on without even realizing it. Go with the flow, I say.

4 With socks, 50% is good enough

No need for undue pressure. Knitting just half the project—that is just one sock—is totally fine. Knitting lots of single socks means never losing the matching sock, and always having another sock to wear.

5 Socks are reassuring

There is something to be said about same old same old. Cuff. Leg. Heel. Foot. Toe. Dr. Benjamin Spock said that routine gives us a sense of security. We know what's coming, we're prepared, and therefore can handle whatever the sock throws at us.

6 Socks are cheekily challenging

But what if you are bored with same old same old and want something to spice things up? Well socks are perfect for this too. Try out a new cast on. Or a different bind off. How about a new heel construction? Or (gasp) steek your sock! There is always a path less traveled if you fancy taking it.

7 Socks are practical

Yes they are. Capital P practical. They keep your feet warm in winter. They help wick away sweat in summer. They cushion your feet as you walk. They help keep your toes from falling off your feet. Hypothermia is a real danger in certain parts of the world.

8 Socks are decorative

Who says socks should be plain black? Lime green, hot pink, fire engine red, brown with cream stripes, pink and gray, orange, purple, blue... you can make them in infinite colors and designs. Express yourself. Go crazy!

9 Socks are subtle

And if you suddenly become all shy, you can always hide your socks in your shoes.

10 Sock knitters rock

I've met loads of awesome, interesting, creative, fun, sweet, lovely, wonderful, funny, and talented sock knitters, many of whom I now count as good friends. And what do I have to thank for all this good fortune? Why, our shared love for hand knit socks, of course!

Chapter 1

Sock Yarn Basics

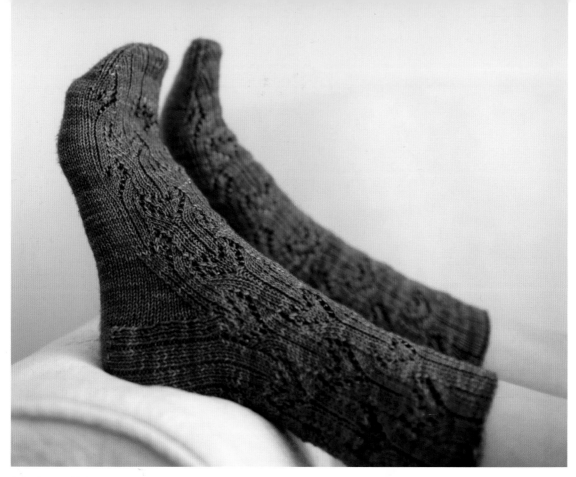

Becoming a sock knitter gains you admission into what feels like an exclusive club of enthusiasts.

What makes a great sock?

A great hand knit sock is born of an ideal combination of fiber and fabric. The aim is to capture the supreme triumvirate: elasticity, strength, and absorbency.

We need elasticity to enable the sock to bounce back to its original form after stretching. A cuff will stretch to twice its size in order to accommodate the heel—it would be disastrous if the sock were to become droopy and baggy after pulling it on.

For the average adult, every step puts about 500 pounds (227kg) of pressure on each foot. In a lifetime, we can expect to walk the equivalent of about three times around Earth's equator. That's a lot of wear and tear on our socks. So a great sock will be able to withstand abrasion from striding along the sidewalks and rubbing inside our shoes.

And though I dislike admitting it, my feet do in fact perspire. Having a sock that is able to absorb the extra moisture and still keep my feet dry and comfy is a quality not to be taken lightly.

Fiber

Fiber is the material used to spin yarn. There are four main types of fiber: cellulose, which comes directly from plants; protein, which comes from animals such as sheep, rabbits, and silkworms; cellulosic, which is plant or protein processed down to a base liquid and then extruded into a spinnable form; and synthetic, which is entirely man-made using artificial materials such as polyester, nylon, and acrylic.

The most prevalent fiber is wool, and it is the fiber I always use for my socks. There isn't any rule saying socks must be made from wool, or cotton, or alpaca, or silk. But taking into consideration the characteristics of fibers and how these feed into the aforementioned triumvirate, the fiber that is most suitable for socks is wool. Cotton lacks elasticity but makes up for it in strength; it is stronger than wool, but not as strong as silk. Cellulosic fibers such as seaweed, bamboo, soy, and corn have varying degrees of absorbency depending on their manufacturing process, but are mostly found in blends with cotton or other protein fibers.

A 100% wool yarn blended with a small amount of nylon (10-20%) gives it a bit more abrasion resistance. Wool can also be blended with other fibers for luxury or sheen-cashmere, silk, alpaca, angora, or mohair, each of which contribute their own unique properties to the finished yarn.

Merino sock yarns

Common Sock Fibers

There are hundreds of different fibers out there, including bamboo, soy, cotton, and corn, which are made into sock yarns. I won't go into all of them here, but if you want to learn more, I heartily recommend Clara Parkes's *The Knitter's Book of Yarn* and Nola Fournier and Jane Fournier's *In Sheep's Clothing* as excellent and indispensable reference books on fiber characteristics.

What we will explore in this section are the most common fibers you will find in sock yarn, and what qualities they bring to the mix.

In order to understand why an animal fiber looks, feels, and acts the way it does, we need to understand three main things: fiber diameter, crimp structure, and staple length.

From sheep to shoe...

A MEASURE OF FINENESS

The finer the fiber, the softer it feels. Cashmere, synonymous with luxury and rub-your-face-in-it softness, is finer than a wool such as Romney. My own scientific softness test, based on years of trial and error, is essentially this: Do I want to hold the yarn to my face and caress it with my cheek? Yes means soft, no means scratchy!

However, I can see that perhaps in a lab with controls and processes, my method may not suit. For the more scientific among us, there are three main grading systems to describe the fineness of fleece: the Blood Count (aka American Count), the micron count, and the Bradford Count (aka English or Spinning Count). The two most popular are the micron count and the Bradford count.

The micron count is the most scientific and straightforward: it is simply the measurement of the diameter of the fiber. One micron is equal to 1/25400th of an inch or 1 millionth of a meter. The lower the micron count, the finer the fleece. To put it into context, cashmere averages about 16 microns, and merino about 20 microns.

The Bradford Count dates back to nineteenth-century England and was named after the city of Bradford where it originated. It is the number of 560-yard (512m) hanks of single ply yarn that can theoretically be spun from one pound of roving. The Bradford Count for any given fleece is a number X followed by the letter "s" for "skeins."

The finer the wool, the more fibers per pound resulting in, theoretically, more skeins that can be spun from one pound of its roving. Merino is

Different staple lengths and crimp in (left to right) mohair, blue-faced leicester, and alpaca.

graded between 80s and 64s, meaning anywhere between 64 and 80 hanks of 560 yards can be spun from one pound of fiber.

CURLS, ZIGZAGS, AND LOCKS

Sheep wool has natural curl; some are tiny wavelets seen best under a microscope, and some are Shirley Temple-like ringlets. More crimp (more waves, zigzags, or curls) means a loftier, springier yarn, which provides better insulation properties as more air is trapped between the fibers. Less crimp makes it easier for individual fibers to lie flat against each other, making a more lustrous and dense, but ultimately less insulating yarn.

LONG HAIR GIVES YOU STRENGTH

Longer fibers spun together will generally form a stronger and more cohesive whole than, all other things being equal, shorter fibers spun together. Longer fibers hold together better when twisted and are less susceptible to pilling since there are fewer fiber ends per inch than with shorter fibers.

In summary: The finer the fiber, the softer it feels against your skin. The more crimp a fiber has, the more bounce, loft, and warmth. Softer fibers tend to also have shorter staple lengths, making them more prone to pilling and less abrasion-resistant. Now let's look at the usual suspects when it comes to sock yarns.

MERINO

If you pop into your local yarn shop, you'll likely find that the most common sock yarn fiber is merino. Merino is the oldest and most numerous established breed in the world. Originally introduced into Spain from North Africa by the Moors, it was so highly prized that exporting breeding stock from Spain was punishable by death! When the Spanish empire began to crumble in the late 1700s, breeding improvement programs began in earnest the world over.

Merino has a high, fine, and even crimp, which gives it excellent insulation properties, loft, and bounce. It averages between 17 and 22 microns. The Australian Wool Corporation provides for three fine grades of merino: Fine at 18.6 to 19.5 microns, Superfine at 15 to 18.5 microns, and Ultrafine at 11.5 to 15 microns, the last two rivaling cashmere in softness.

Despite merino's relatively short staple length of between 2.5 and 4 inches (1 and 10cm), it has a high tensile strength. Spinning and plying the short fibers more tightly helps increase durability; you'll find that the best sock yarns made from merino have a very tight twist.

BLUE-FACED LEICESTER

These distinctive looking sheep with their Roman noses originated near Hexham in Northumberland in the early 1900s. They are called "blue faced" not because they are blue, but rather because their black skin seen through their white fleece gives them a blue hue. BFL, as they are commonly known, resulted from selective breeding pioneered by Robert Bakewell, an influential eighteenth-century farmer.

The long staple—3 to 6 inches (7.5 to 15cm)—and a relatively fine micron count (24 to 28) result in a nice balance between softness and durability, making it a popular wool among hand knitters. It takes dye beautifully and has a reflective quality that makes it a favorite with hand dyers. It has an open loose crimp, which produces a lustrous yarn, though one that's less insulating than a fiber with higher crimp. BFL has one of the softest fibers of native English sheep, and is perfectly suited for next-to-skin wear.

ALPACA

Alpacas originate from the Andean highlands of South America and can be categorised into two main types: Huacaya, which look like big fluffy teddy bears, and Suri, which produce long silky dreadlock-like coats and account for only 10% of the current alpaca population.

Good quality alpaca fiber averages 18 to 26 microns and has a long staple ranging from $4\frac{1}{2}$ to 11 inches (11.5 to 28cm) or longer, depending on how often they have been shorn. Because the fibers are mostly hollow, alpaca has a very high warmth-to-weight ratio—three times warmer than sheep's wool. It also has a high tensile strength that makes for durable garments. Since alpacas don't secrete lanolin, their fiber is suitable for those allergic to sheep's wool.

However, if using 100% alpaca yarn for socks be aware that, because the fiber is very dense and has no memory, the sock is likely to give in to gravity sooner rather than later; without the necessary elasticity, the sock won't readily bounce back to its original shape. The secret to enjoying the warmth and durability of alpaca fiber in socks is to blend it with a fiber that has better elasticity.

MOHAIR

Mohair comes from the angora goat. Angora, on the other hand, comes from cute fluffy magical bunnies (okay, not really magical but cute and fluffy, most definitely) called angora rabbits and has nothing to do with the angora goat, other than also being cute.

Mohair is an excellent fiber to add to sock yarn because it has a nice long staple length (3 to 6 inches/7.5 to 15 cm), making it extremely durable; in fact it has all three characteristics of the best sock yarn—elasticity, strength, and absorbency. The only thing that keeps it from being the crown prince of socks is the fact that it can bloom significantly; furry socks have yet to become a trending fashion item.

CASHMERE

If I could, I would wrap myself in cashmere 24/7. This lovely, but expensive, fiber comes from the undercoat of a goat, the *Capra hircus laniger*, otherwise known as the cashmere goat.

If you have deduced that such a soft fiber must have a short staple, you are correct. Cashmere fiber averages 1¼ to 3½ inches (3 to 9 cm) in staple length and 16 microns in diameter. It is more than 30% lighter than wool and eight times warmer. Thankfully, a little bit goes a long way, which is why yarn with just 10% or 20% cashmere feels so wonderful.

There is no denying that a cashmere garment is a delicate creature more suited to pampering and indulgence than to pounding the pavements. I wouldn't advise that you wear cashmere socks out jogging, as a friend of mine once did and then wondered why she found a big hole in the heel when she got home. But if you feel the need to luxuriate in something while lounging about in bed or perhaps in a silk robe on a divan, you can't go wrong with cashmere.

Opposite **Pure cashmere fiber**

SILK

Silk is produced from the fibroin filament secreted by a silkworm and used to spin its cocoon. One little silkworm secretes some 800 yards (732m) of fibroin. It is one of the strongest natural fibers around. The fiber has a triangular prism-like structure that refracts light at different angles, giving the shimmering effect we associate with silk. It does have a few drawbacks, and if you've ever worn a silk skirt or shirt, you know that silk is very susceptible to static cling (being a poor conductor of electricity), and has little elasticity of its own. It loses up to 20% of its strength when wet and if you stretch it, it stays stretched. Too much sun will weaken the fibers (but it will not spontaneously burst into flame like a vampire). When blended, it will lend its reflective qualities and its strength to the whole. It's a nice addition to a sock yarn that needs a little glitz and shine.

Yarn Construction

PLIES

Yarn is fiber that has been spun into strands (also called plies), which, except for singles yarn, are then plied together. The degree of twist spun into the strands and the degree of twist used when the strands are plied together can vary.

A singles yarn has only one strand, a 2-ply yarn has two strands twisted together, 3-ply yarn has three strands, 4-ply has four strands, and so on. For cabled yarns, a multiple of 2+ plies twisted together are plied together. Cashmere is often cabled as it results in a stronger yarn. The general rule of thumb is the more strands twisted together, the stronger the yarn.

TWIST

A good twist gives yarn bounce and energy. With sock yarns, a tight twist provides increased abrasion resistance, though sock yarns with a looser twist can also be made more abrasion-resistant by knitting at a tighter gauge.

Opposite Socktopus Sokkusu Original, a light fingering yarn made of 3 plies

Sock Yarns from Around the World

All sock yarn is just sock yarn, isn't it? Well, yes and no. Sock yarn is really just yarn that is thin enough for socks, and depending on the kind of sock you are after, the yarn could be lace weight, sport weight, or even thicker and chunkier for thick cushy hiking socks. But for the majority of sock patterns, the most common yarn used is fingering weight.

YARN WEIGHT COMPARISONS

You'll often hear sock yarn referred to as "fingering weight" or "3-ply" yarn. These two weights are actually different—3-ply is thinner than fingering weight. The USA, the UK, and Australia all use different terminology to describe a certain weight of yarn, so it can certainly get confusing. To help clarify, the following table shows the common weights of yarn used to knit socks and their international equivalents.

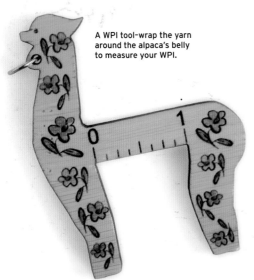

A WPI tool-wrap the yarn around the alpaca's belly to measure your WPI.

USA	UK	AUSTRALIA	WPI
Light fingering	3-ply	3-ply	16
Fingering	4-ply	4-ply	14
Sport	Light DK	5-ply	12

WRAPS PER INCH (WPI)

An easy way of classifying the thickness of your yarn is by measuring its wraps per inch (WPI). This is the method used by spinners to determine yarn weight. To calculate WPI, wrap the yarn gently around an inch ruler. The yarn should not be pulled tight, but should sit flat against the ruler. Count how many wraps for that inch, and that's the WPI.

GAUGE AND SIZE

If there is a specific yarn you want to use for a pattern but the yarn gauge doesn't match the pattern gauge, you need to adjust the measurements from the pattern to avoid getting either huge or teeny socks. Follow this rule of thumb: using a thicker yarn (and the yarn's own ideal gauge) will result in a larger sock since less stitches are required to make the same inch of fabric. For example, Shur'tugal has a gauge of 9sts/inch (2.5cm). The leg circumference uses 64st and 72st (giving 7 and 8 inches/18 and 20cm respectively). To substitute a yarn with a gauge of 8st per inch (2.5cm), and a desired leg circumference of 8 inches (20cm), then knitting the smaller size would give the right size, since 8 sts/inch (2.5cm) x 8 inches (20cm) = 64 sts.

These are swatches of different yarns with different numbers of plies and fibre composition. Some feel thicker than others due to the weight of the yarn; it's worth knitting up your own swatch library so you will know how a yarn will behave at a given gauge, and whether you will like the resulting fabric.

2-PLY

(*Clockwise from top left*)

a) Crown Mountain Farms Sock Hop Yarn "Layla" handspun 100% Superwash Merino

b) Fyberspates Sheilas Gold Sparkle sock "Purple", 75% Superwash Merino, 20% Nylon, 5% GOLD Stellina

c) Madelinetosh Sock "Logwood" 100% Superwash Merino

d) Koigu KPPPM "P90561" 100% Merino Wool

e) Green Mountain Spinnery Sock Art-Meadow "Pink" 50% Wool 50% Mohair

3-PLY

(*Top to bottom*)

a) Dream in Color Smooshy "Wisterious" 100% Superwash Merino

b) Shelridge Farm Soft Touch Ultra "Green Apple" 100% Wool

c) Sokkusu Original "JWM's WInd Rain and Wool" 100% Superwash Merino

3-PLY

(Clockwise from top left)

a) Hazelknits Artisan Sock "Olympic Rainforest" 90% Merino 10% Nylon

b) Spirit Trail Fiberworks Sunna "Antique Tapestry" 75% Merino 15% Cashmere 10% Bombyx Silk

c) Socktopus Sokkusu Xtra "Corallina" 70% Superwash Merino 20% Cashmere 10% Nylon

d) Colinette Jitterbug "Elephant's Daydream" 100% Merino

e) Blue Moon Fiber Arts Socks That Rock "Goody Goody" 100% Merino

4+-PLY

(Clockwise from top left)

a) Lorna's Laces Shepherd Sock "Bleen and Grue" 80% Merino 20% Nylon (4 ply)

b) Easyknits Bamboo-Merino "Luau" 80% Merino 20% Bamboo (4 ply)

c) Wollmeise 100% Merino Superwash "Edelstein" 100% Merino Superwash (9 ply)

d) Alchemy Juniper "Rumplestiltskin" 100% Merino (6 ply)

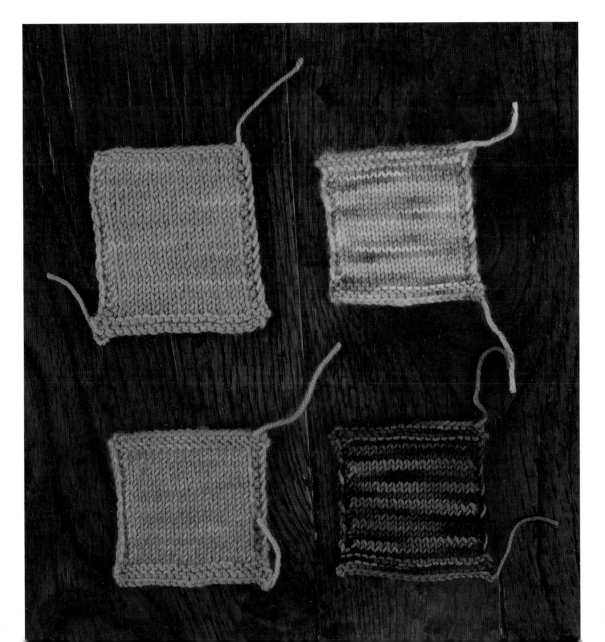

Sock Fit and Anatomy

SOCK FIT

There are two golden rules you need to follow to get great-fitting socks:

1. Take proper measurements

2. Use appropriate negative ease.

Two measurements are key:

1. Foot circumference

2. Foot length.

The circumference of the foot should be taken around the ball of the foot. This is roughly the same as the ankle measurement and determines the number of stitches used in the leg. The sock will stretch to accommodate the increased girth of the leg from calf muscles; from the ankle down, gusset shaping provides the extra space needed for the instep. The second measurement is the foot length from the back of the heel to the tip of the longest toe.

It is crucial to incorporate negative ease when calculating the circumference and length of the sock. A sock made to the exact measurements of the foot will be ill-fitting and floppy. Incorporating an inch (2.5cm) (that is, about 10% of the total measurement) of negative ease will force the sock to stretch and hug the contours of the foot for a perfect fit. Totally Vanilla (page 32) puts these rules into practice. Not everyone's foot will measure out perfectly – some will have larger ankles, some smaller. If the negative ease is too much, the sock will be uncomfortably tight. Increasing the girth of the leg or the foot can accommodate this, and gusset shaping can take up any extra stitches used for custom sizing.

Note: On all the patterns in this book, the measurements included on the diagrams are the size of the finished sock blocked but unstretched.

SOCK ANATOMY

(See diagram opposite)

Cuff: Usually ribbed to help keep the sock up, but not strictly necessary as enough negative ease will keep the sock from falling.

Leg: Normally the number of stitches on the leg will match the number of stitches on the foot after gusset shaping. This number is based on the measurement around the ball of your foot or your ankle circumference.

Heel: This can be a short row heel, which does not interrupt the lines of striping yarns, or a heel flap. Using a slip-stitch pattern will reinforce the heel against abrasion.

Gusset: This is the area of the sock that makes way for the instep. To accommodate a higher instep, a heel flap can be made longer, or a short row heel can be worked on 60% of the stitches rather than the usual 50%. There are numerous ways of incorporating gusset shaping. The traditional manner has mirrored shaping both sides of the foot. More explorative shaping is asymmetric, or in one specific area such as the bottom of the foot, the top, or the back of the leg.

Toe: There are innumerable ways of shaping the toe: star toe, wedge toe, form-fitting asymmetric toes. The world is your toe oyster.

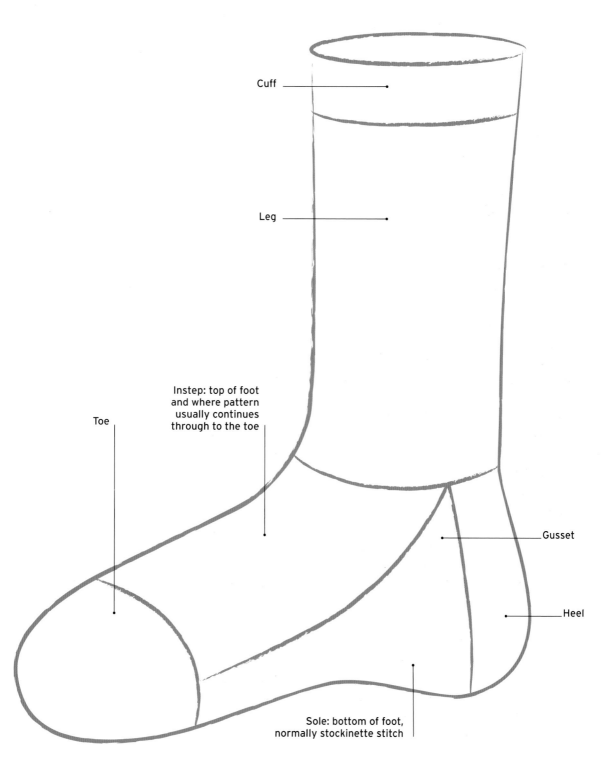

Cuff

Leg

Instep: top of foot
and where pattern
usually continues
through to the toe

Toe

Gusset

Heel

Sole: bottom of foot,
normally stockinette stitch

Chapter 2

The Patterns

Totally Vanilla

There are times when you just want to sit with friends knitting something that isn't at all taxing. Here's my Totally Vanilla sock, which is great for times when my brain isn't quite up to the task of remembering stitch patterns, or when I fancy doing some knitting, but also really fancy having a drink with some friends. When K.U.I. (Knitting Under the Influence), stockinette stitch is my friend.

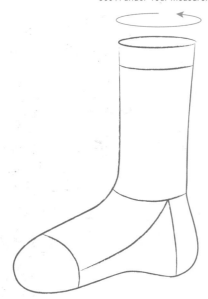

See A under Your measurements

SOCK VITALS

Your measurements

Measure your foot

A: Foot circumference _____ inches (cm)

B: Foot length _____ inches (cm)

Yarn

Your choice. As a general guide here is the expected gauge for the three most common sock yarn weights:

12 WPI = 32 sts over 4in (10cm) in stockinette stitch

14 WPI = 36 sts over 4in (10cm) in stockinette stitch

16 WPI = 40 sts over 4in (10cm) in stockinette stitch

Needles

Choose needles that will give you the correct gauge for your yarn. We each have our own personal knitting style—some knit tightly, some knit loosely—so you'll need to choose needles to achieve a certain gauge.

Your gauge

Using the appropriate gauge for your yarn, calculate the number of sts per inch (2.5cm) of St st by dividing the number of sts over 4 inches by 4 inches (10 x 10cm). Write it down next to C.

C _____ sts/inch (2.5cm)

Negative ease

A well-fitting sock is usually 1 inch (2.5cm) narrower and shorter than actual foot measurements, but you can adjust this to your preference.

Foot circumference

To calculate the number of stitches to cast on, first calculate the sock circumference, which will be 1 inch (2.5cm) smaller than your actual foot circumference.

A _____ - 1 inch (2.5cm) = Negative Ease Circumference D _____.

Multiply the negative ease circumference by the number of sts per inch (2.5cm) from your gauge (C) to get the total number of stitches to cast on.

D _____ x C _____ = number of stitches to cast on = X _____.

The number of sts must be divisible by 4, so round up or down, whichever is the closest.

Foot length

Subtract 1 inch (2.5cm) from your actual foot length to get the desired length for the foot of the sock (E):

B _____ - 1 inch (2.5cm) = E _____.

When you knit the foot you will have to decrease for the toe. This will happen 1½ inches (4cm) before the end of the sock foot. Subtract 1½ inches (4cm) from E, the desired length of the sock to get Z, the place to start toe decreases.

E _____ - 1½ inch (4cm) = Z _____.

CUFF

Cast on X sts. Work ribbing for 1 inch (2.5cm).

LEG

Work St st until leg is desired length, ending just above the ankle bone.

HEEL

Work the heel flap over the first half of the sts. The second half of the sts are held for the instep.

Row 1: K first half of sts
(X divided by 2 = F _____).
Row 2: (Sl1, p1) to end of row.
Row 3: Sl1, k to end of row.

Rep rows 2 and 3 fourteen times more. If you have a higher instep, then you can make your heel flap longer for a better fit.

Heel turn

Divide the number of heel sts by 2.
Subtract 1. This number is Y.
(F divided by 2 – 1 = Y _____).

Row 1: (WS) Sl1, pY, p2, p2tog, p1, turn.
Row 2: Sl1, k4, ssk, k1, turn.
Row 3: Sl1, p5 (purling to 1 st before gap), p2tog, p1, turn.
Row 4: Sl1, k6 (knitting to 1 st before gap), ssk, k1, turn.
Cont in this manner until no sts rem after gap, ending with a RS row. You may have to end with an ssk without the k1. Do not turn.

GUSSET

If you made a longer heel flap, simply pick up additional stitches on each side of the heel flap. Make sure you pick up the same number of stitches on each side.

Tip: Here's an easy way to close the gap that sometimes forms between heel flap and instep sts. When working the gusset pick-up round, pick up and knit an extra st in the gap between the heel flap and instep sts before and after the instep sts. On the following round, work the first extra st together with the first instep st as a k2tog and work the second extra st together with the last instep st as an ssk.

Round 1: Pick up and k1 st in each of the slipped sts down the side of the heel flap, pm, k the held instep sts, pm, pick up and k1 st in each of the slipped sts up the side of the heel flap, pm, k to end of round.
Round 2: Ktbl to within 2 sts of marker, k2tog, sm, k to marker, sm, ssk, ktbl to marker, sm, k to end.
Round 3: Knit.
Round 4: K to within 2 sts of marker, k2tog, sm, k to marker, sm, ssk, k to marker, sm, k to end.
Rep rounds 3 and 4 until original number of stitches is restored, ending with round 3.

FOOT

Set up: K to marker, sm, k to marker, remove marker. New start of round.
Cont knitting in St st until work measures length Z.
(E – 1½ inches (4cm) = Z _____).

TOE

Round 1: K1, ssk, k to within 3 sts of marker, k2tog, k1, sm, k1, ssk, k to last 3 sts, k2tog, k1 (4 sts decreased).
Round 2: Knit.
Rep rounds 1 and 2 until approximately 40 sts rem, then rep round 1 only until approximately 10 sts rem.

FINISHING

Cut yarn, leaving an 8in (20cm) tail. With tail threaded on a tapestry needle, graft toe shut. Weave in ends.

Kandahar

There is nothing quite like swooshing down a beautiful piste of freshly packed snow. These zippy socks have downhill pistes winding their way down the leg, and a central panel of tractor-groomed snow. Named after the oldest downhill ski race, these are aprés-ski socks to be worn while sitting next to a crackling fire with Testarossa cocktail in hand.

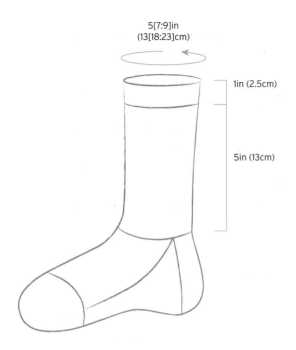

5[7:9]in
(13[18:23]cm)

1in (2.5cm)

5in (13cm)

SOCK VITALS

Yarn
Sokkusu Lightweight 100% superwash merino
(472yds/432m per 100g):
1 skein in Midsommer

Needles
US 1.5 (2.5mm) or size needed to obtain
correct gauge

Gauge
36 sts to 4in (10cm) over stockinette stitch

Notions
Stitch markers
Tapestry needle

CUFF
Cast on 48[64, 80] sts.
Round 1 *K4, (p2, k2) 5[7:9] times, pm, rep
from * once more.
Round 2 *P2, (k2, p2) 5[7:9] times, k2, sm, rep
from * once more.
Rep rounds 1 and 2 six times more.

LEG
Work Leg Chart until leg measures 6in (15cm)
from top of cuff, ending with row 16[12:16] of
Leg Chart.

Medium size only
Work rows 1 to 4 of Heel Set-up Chart.

HEEL
The heel is now worked flat over the first
13[17:21] sts and the last 11[15:19] sts of the
round. The remaining sts are held for the
instep.

Set-up row: Work Set-up row from Heel Flap
Chart, turn.
Row 1: (WS) Work row 1 of Heel Flap Chart, turn.
Row 2: (RS) Work row 2 of Heel Flap Chart, turn.
Rows 3-10: Continue working Heel Flap Chart
as set.

Small and medium sizes
Rep rows 9 and 10 six[nine] times more.

Large size only
Rep rows 17 and 18 ten times more.

Heel turn

Row 1: (WS) Sl1, p12[18:23], p2tog, p1, turn.
Row 2: (RS) Sl1, k3[7:7], ssk, k1, turn.
Row 3: Sl1, p4[8:8], p2tog, p1, turn.
Row 4: Sl1, k5[9:9], ssk, k1, turn.

Small size

Rows 5-9: Continue as set.
Row 10: (RS) Sl1, k11, ssk, k1, do not turn (14 heel sts).

Medium size

Rows 5-11: Continue as set.
Row 12: (RS) Sl1, k17, ssk, k1, do not turn (20 heel sts).

Large size

Rows 5-15: Continue as set.
Row 16: (RS) Sl1, k21, ssk, k1, do not turn (24 heel sts).

All sizes

Resume working in the round.

GUSSET

Round 1: Pick up and k1 st in each slipped st down the side of the heel flap (12[15:20] sts picked up, k0[1:0] from the held instep sts, pm, work row 1 of Instep Chart, pm, k0[1:0], pick up and k1 st in each slipped st up the side of the heel flap (12[15:20] sts picked up), k7[10:12]. New start of round.
Round 2: K7[10:12], k10[14:28] tbl, k2tog, sm, work row 2 of Instep Chart, sm, ssk, k10[14:18] tbl, k7[10:12].
Round 3: K to marker, sm, continue working Instep Chart as set, sm, k to end.

Round 4: K to within 2 sts of marker, k2tog, sm, continue working Instep Chart as set, sm, ssk, k to end.
Rep rounds 3 and 4 until 48[60:80] sts rem (12[15:20] before first marker, 24[30:40] between markers, and 12[15:20] to end).
Rearrange sts as follows:
K to marker. New start of round. The first 24[30:40] sts are the instep sts, worked in pattern. The rem sts are the sole sts and are worked in St st.

FOOT

Round 1: Continue working Instep Chart as set, sm, k to end.
Rep round 1 until foot measures 1½ in[2:2½ in] (4[5:6.5] cm) less than desired length, ending with row 12[4:12] of Instep Chart.

TOE

Work Toe Chart over instep sts and St st over sole sts until row 8[10:8] of Toe Chart has been worked.

Continue from row 9[11:9] of Toe Chart on instep sts, mirroring the decreases from the Toe Chart at the beg and end of the sole sts; the sole sts should all begin with k1, ssk, and end with k2tog, k1 over a St st background.
At end of Toe Chart, 16 sts remain.

FINISHING

Cut yarn, leaving an 8in (20cm) tail. With tail threaded on a tapestry needle, graft toe shut. Weave in ends.

Leg Chart

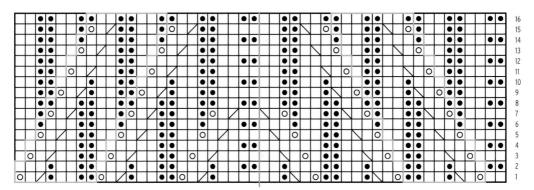

Heel Set-up Chart

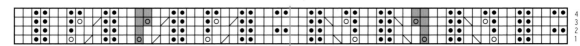

CHART KEY

▢▢ center marker		● purl on RS, knit on WS	
╱ k2tog on RS, p2tog on WS		V slip	
▢ knit on RS, purl on WS		╲ ssk	
▨ no stitch		⊙ yo	
▢ pattern repeat			

Heel Flap Chart—large

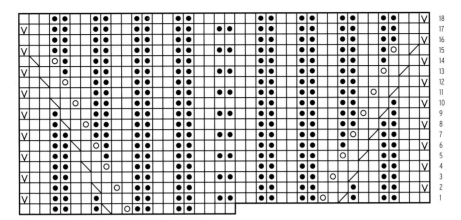

Heel Flap Chart—medium

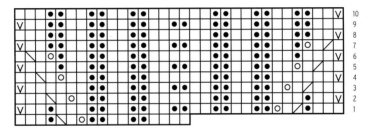

Heel Flap Chart—small

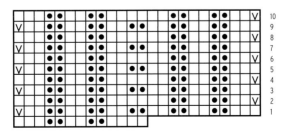

Instep Chart—large

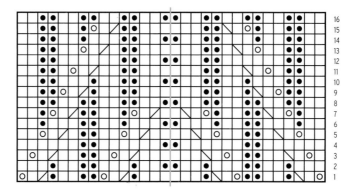

Instep Chart—medium

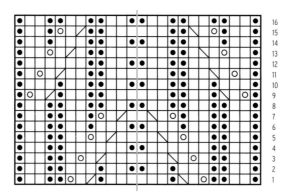

Instep Chart—small

Toe Chart–large

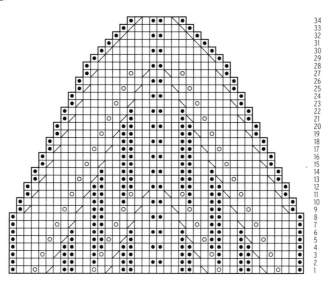

Toe Chart–medium

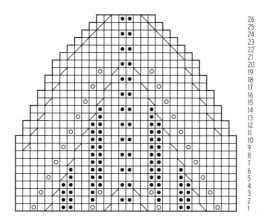

Toe Chart–small

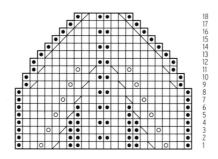

V Junkie

Red blood cells made from slipped stitches and purl rows, these socks were inspired by *True Blood*, a TV series based on the Sookie Stackhouse novels written by Charlaine Harris. V junkies are vampire blood addicts. Like they say in the series, one drop is all it takes...

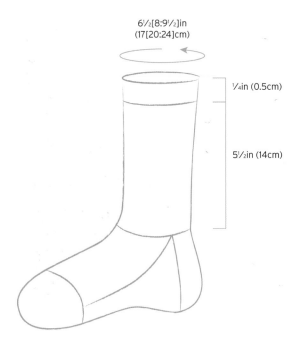

6½[8:9½]in
(17[20:24]cm)

¼in (0.5cm)

5½in (14cm)

SOCK VITALS

Yarn

Sokkusu Original 100% superwash merino
(433yds/396m per 120g):
1 skein in Lost Meadow

Needles

US1.5 (2.5mm) or size needed to obtain
correct gauge

Gauge

36 sts to 4in (10 cm) over stockinette stitch

Notions

Tapestry needle

Technique note

WT (wrap and turn): Bring yarn forward,
slip the next stitch, bring yarn back, return
the slipped stitch to the left needle, then
turn the work.

CUFF

Cast on 60[72:84] sts and join for knitting in
the round.

Round 1: K3, sl1, *k5, sl1, rep from * to last
2 sts, k2.

Round 2: P3, sl1, *p5, sl1, rep from * to last
2 sts, p2.

Round 3: Purl.

LEG

Round 1: *Sl1, k5, rep from * to end.

Rounds 2-7: Rep round 1.

Rounds 8 and 9: Purl.

Round 10: K3, sl1, *k5, sl1, rep from * to last
2 sts, k2.

Rounds 11-16: Rep round 10.

Rounds 17 and 18: Purl.

These 18 rows set leg cell pattern. Rep rounds
1 through 18 of leg cell pattern 5 times more.

HEEL

Set-up round: *Sl1, k5, rep from * 4[5:6] times
more, sl1.

The heel is worked flat from this point over the
next 29[35:41] sts. The sts just worked are held
for the instep.

Row 1: (RS) K to last st, WT.

Row 2: (WS) K to last st, WT (1 wrapped st
either side).

Row 3: K to last unwrapped st, WT.

Row 4: K to last unwrapped st, WT (2 wrapped sts either side).

Cont working short rows as set in rows 3 and 4 until there are 10[13:16] wrapped sts either side, and 9 unwrapped sts in the middle, ending with a WS row.

Heel turn

Row 1: (RS) K9 to first wrapped st, WT (the st just wrapped is now double wrapped).

Row 2: K9 to first wrapped st, WT (the st just wrapped is now double wrapped).

Row 3: K10 to first single wrapped st, WT.

Row 4: K11 to first single wrapped st, WT (2 double wrapped sts either side).

Row 5: K12, WT.

Row 6: K13, WT (3 double wrapped sts either side).

Cont in this manner until all wrapped sts have been double wrapped, ending with a WS row.

FOOT

Note on fit: The forefoot adds 1½[2:2½]in (4[5:6.5]cm) in addition to the toe shaping, so be sure to allow for that when calculating how much of the foot pattern to work.

The sock is now knit in the round again, RS facing. The first 31[37:43] sts are the instep sts, the remaining 29[35:41] sts are the sole sts.

Set-up: K29[35:41]. New start of round.

Round 1: *Sl1, k5, rep from * 4[5:6] times more, sl1, pm, k to end.

Round 2: *Sl1, k5, rep from * to within 1 st of marker, sl1, sm, k to end.

Rounds 3-6: Rep round 2.

Rounds 7 and 8: P to marker, sm, k to end.

Round 9: K3, sl1, *k5, sl1, rep from * to within 3 sts of marker, k3, sm, k to end.

Rounds 10-15: Rep round 9.

Rounds 16 and 17: P to marker, sm, k to end.

Round 18: Rep round 2.

Cont working rounds 1 to 18 as set over the instep, and working the sole in St st until foot measures 3[4:5]in (7.5[10:12.5]cm) less than desired finished length (see note on fit), ending with round 15.

Forefoot

Round 1: K3, p to within 3 sts of marker, k3, sm, k to end.

Round 2: Rep round 1.

Round 3: K6, sl1, *k5, sl1, rep from * to within 6 sts of marker, k6, sm, k to end.

Rounds 4-9: Rep round 3.

Round 10: K6, p to within 6 sts of marker, k6, sm, k to end.

Round 11: Rep round 10.

Round 12: K9, sl1, *k5, sl1, rep from * to within 9 sts of marker, k9, sm, k to end.

Rounds 13-18: Rep round 12.

Round 19: K9, p to within 9 sts of marker, k9, sm, k to end.

Round 20: Rep round 19.

Round 21: K12, sl1, *k5, sl1, rep from * to within 12 sts of marker, k12, sm, k to end.

Rounds 22-27: Rep round 21.

Round 28: K12, p to within 12 sts of marker, k12, sm, k to end.

Round 29: Rep round 28.

Medium and large sizes only

Round 30: K15, sl1, *k5, sl1, rep from * to within 15 sts of marker, k15, sm, k to end.

Rounds 31-36: Rep round 30.

Round 37: K15, p to within 15 sts of marker, k15, sm, k to end.

Round 38: Rep round 37.

Large size only

Round 39: K18, sl1, k5, sl1, k18, sm, k to end.

Rounds 40-45: Rep round 39.

Round 46: K18, p7, k18, sm, k to end.

Round 47: Rep round 46.

TOE

Round 1: K1, ssk, k12[15:18], sl1, k12[15:18], k2tog, k1, sm, k to end (29[35:41] instep sts, 29[35:41] sole sts).

Round 2: K14[17:20], sl1, k to end.

Round 3: K1, ssk, k to within 3 sts of marker, k2tog, k1, sm, k1, ssk, k to last 3 sts, k2tog, k1.

Round 4: Knit.

Cont to dec 4 sts on every alt round as set until 38 sts rem.

Rep round 3 only until 6 sts rem.

FINISHING

Cut yarn, leaving an 8in (20cm) tail. With tail threaded on a tapestry needle, graft toe shut. Weave in ends.

Kwalla

Like all 13-year-old girls (what? Well maybe 30... something...)
I was obsessed for a time with the *Twilight* books. I've grown
up and moved on... but out of girlish devotion, I named these
socks after the mighty whale in Quileute legends, the Native
American tribe featured in the book. The cables and
swirls are like water churned by a diving whale
heading back to its underwater realm.

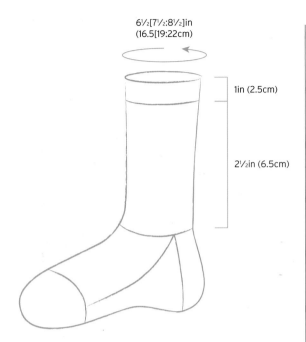

6½[7½:8½]in
(16.5[19:22cm)

1in (2.5cm)

2½in (6.5cm)

SOCK VITALS

Yarn
Sokkusu Original 100% superwash merino
(433yds/396m per 120g):
1 skein in Man of Rock

Needles
US 1.5 (2.5mm) or size needed to obtain
correct gauge

Gauge
36 sts to 4in (10cm) in stockinette stitch
44 sts to 4in (10cm) in pattern

Notions
Stitch markers
Tapestry needle

Technique notes

ksw (knit shadow wrap): Using the right
needle tip, lift the top of the stitch (the
"mama" stitch) below the first stitch (the
"daughter" stitch) on the left needle. **1**
Place the mama stitch on the left needle, **2**
being careful not to twist it. Knit the mama
stitch to make a "shadow" stitch **3** and
drop the mama stitch off the left needle. **4**
Slip the daughter stitch from the left needle
to the right needle. **5** You now have two
loops coming out of the mama stitch–the
daughter stitch and the shadow stitch, which
are worked together as a single stitch.

c6b (cable 6 back): Slip 3 sts to cable
needle and hold to back, k3 from left
needle, k3 from cable needle.

c6f (cable 6 front): Slip 3 sts to cable
needle and hold to front, k3 from left
needle, k3 from cable needle.

CUFF
Cast on 72[84:96] sts. Join to work in the round
being careful not to twist sts.
Round 1: *K2, p1, k2, p1, k3, p2, k1, rep from *
5[6:7] times more.
Rep round 1 until rib measures 1in (2.5cm).

LEG
Round 1: Work row 1 of Leg Chart 6[7:8] times
Round 2: Work row 2 of Leg Chart 6[7:8] times.
Rounds 3 to 18: Cont working Leg Chart as set.

Knit shadow wrap

1

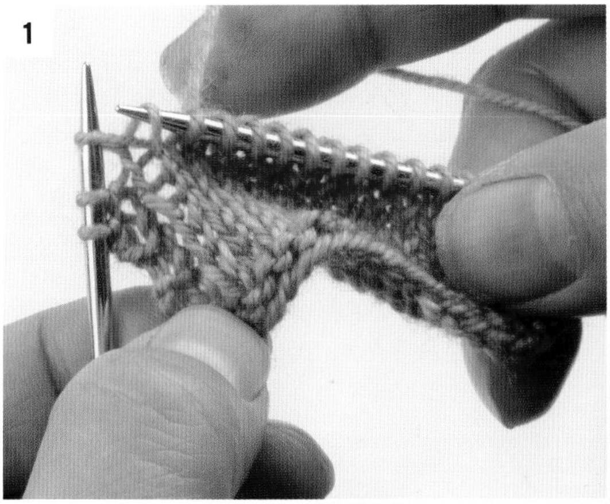

2

3

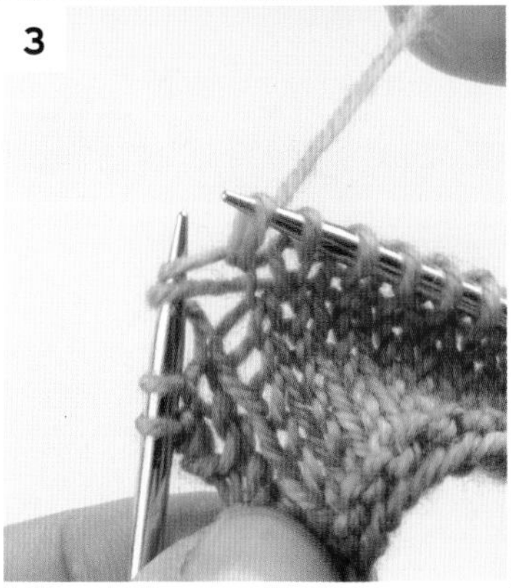

4

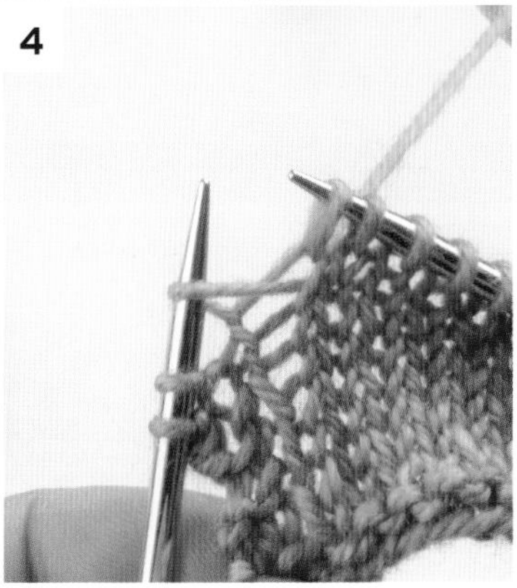

5

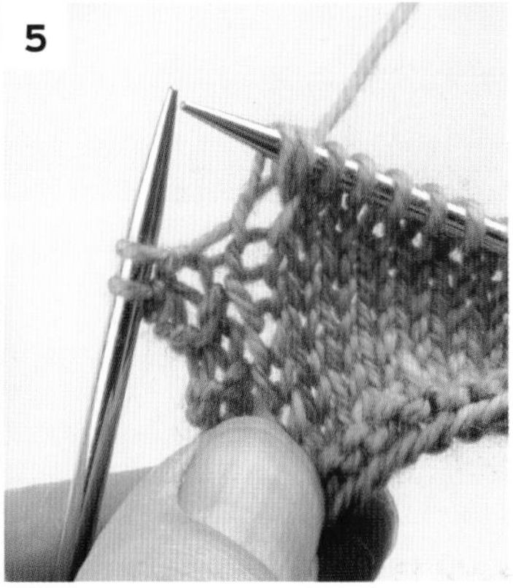

Rep rows 7 through 18 of Leg Chart until work measures 4in (10cm) from cast-on edge, ending with row 11 or 17. Make a note of the row you ended with.

HEEL

The heel is worked flat on the first 36[42:48] sts, the rem sts are held for the instep.

Row 1: (RS) K36[42:48], turn.
Row 2: (WS) *Sl1, p1, rep from * to end.
Row 3: Sl1, k to end.
Rep rows 2 and 3 fourteen times more.

Heel turn

Row 1: (WS) Sl1, p20[22:26], psw, turn.
Row 2: (RS) Sl1, k6[4:6] ksw.
Row 3: Sl1, p to twin st, p twin st, p1, psw.
Row 4: Sl1, k to twin st, k twin st, k1, ksw.
Rep rows 3 and 4 until all sts have been worked, finishing with a RS row.

GUSSET DECREASES

Return to working in the round.

Round 1: Pick up and k15 sts down the side of the heel flap, pm, k36[42:48] across instep, pm, pick up and k15 sts down the other side of the heel flap 102[114:126] sts).

Small and large sizes

Round 2: K to 2 sts before marker, k2tog, sm, continue working Leg Chart as set across instep to marker, sm, ssk, k to end of round.

Medium size only

Round 2: K to within 2 sts of marker, k2tog, sm, work Instep Chart (see note below) to marker, sm, ssk, k to end of round.
Note for medium size only: If you ended with Row 11 before the heel, start with Row 7 of the

Technique note

psw (purl shadow wrap): Slip next stitch purlwise to right needle. **1** With the left needle, lift the top of the mama stitch of the stitch you just placed on the right needle being careful not to twist it. **2** Purl the mama stitch to make a new shadow stitch. **3** You now have a daughter stitch and a shadow stitch coming out of the mama stitch. When you work the stitch and its shadow, treat them as a single stitch.

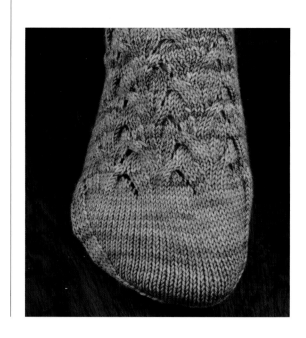

Purl shadow wrap

instep chart. If you ended with Row 17 before the heel, start with Row 1 of the Instep Chart.

All sizes

Round 3: K to marker, sm, continue working in pattern across instep to marker as established on round 2, sm, k to end of round.

Rep rounds 2 and 3 until 72[84:96] sts rem.

Rep round 3 until sock measures 1[1½:2]in (2.5[4:5]cm) less than desired finished length measured from heel of sock, ending with row 12 or 18 of the Leg Chart for small and large sizes or row 6 or 12 of Instep Chart for medium size.

TOE

Round 1: K to marker, new start of round.

Round 2: K1, ssk, k to within 3 sts of marker, k2tog, k1, sm, k1, ssk, k to last 3 sts, k2tog, k1.

Round 3: Knit.

Rep rounds 2 and 3 until 40 sts rem. Rep round 2 until 12 sts rem.

FINISHING

Cut yarn, leaving an 8in (20cm) tail. With tail threaded on a tapestry needle, graft toe shut. Weave in ends.

Leg Chart

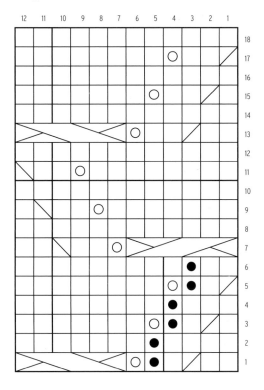

CHART KEY

 ssk

knit

k2tog

● purl

 C6b

C6f

○ yo

pattern repeat

Instep Chart

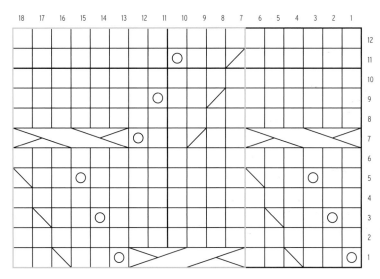

Farmer McGregor

I very rarely knit socks for my husband since he

is quite picky. These socks, however, got the thumbs-up.

Nothing too fancy or frilly here, just nice manly geometric

shapes with enough complexity to keep it interesting.

The texture is also perfect for variegated yarns.

7[8:9] in
(18[20:23]cm)

1in (2.5cm)

5½in (14cm)

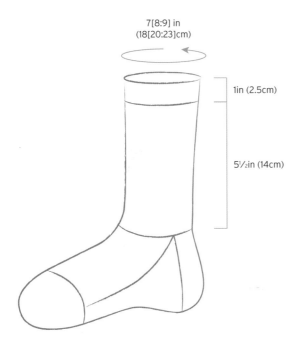

SOCK VITALS

Yarn
Sokkusu Original 100% superwash merino
(433yds/396m per 120g):
1 skein in Prairie Dog

Needles
US 1.5 (2.5mm) or size needed to obtain
correct gauge

Gauge
36 sts to 4in (10cm) in stockinette stitch

Notions
Tapestry needle

Technique notes

LT (left twist): Slip 2 sts knitwise one at a
time, and slip both back onto left needle. **1**
With the right needle, knit into the back of
the second st, **2** leaving the st on the left
needle, **3** then knit into the back of both
the first and second sts and drop both
from the left needle. **4**
RT (right twist): K2tog, leaving sts on left
hand needle; **1** with the right needle, knit
into first st again (the st closest to the tip of
the left needle), **2** and drop both sts from
left needle. **3**

CUFF
Cast on 64[72:80] sts. Join to work in the round
being careful not to twist sts.
Round 1: K1, *p2, k2, rep from * to last 3 sts, p2,
k1. Rep round 1 until rib measures 1in (2.5cm).

Left twist (top) and right twist (bottom)

1

2

3

4

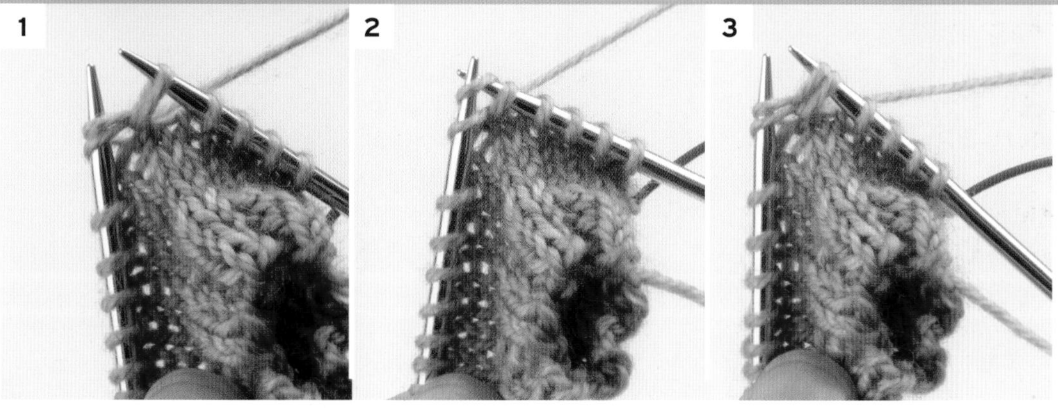

1

2

3

LEG
Set-up
Round 1: *K1, p1, RT, LT, p1, k1, rep from * to end.
Round 2: *K1, p1, k4, p1, k1, rep from * to end.
Round 3: *K1, RT, k2, LT, k1, rep from * to end.

Begin pattern
Round 1: Knit.
Round 2: *(RT) twice, (LT) twice, rep from * to end.
Round 3: Knit.
Round 4: Sl1, *RT, k2, LT, RT, rep from * to last 7 sts, RT, k2, LT, move slipped st from start of round from left needle to right needle, RT.
Round 5: K to 1 st before end. This is the new start of round.
Round 6: *RT, k4, RT, rep from * to end.
Round 7: Knit.
Round 8: Sl1, *LT, k2, (RT) twice, rep from * to last 7 sts, LT, k2, RT, move slipped st from start of round from left needle to right needle, RT.
Round 9: Knit to 1 st before end. This is the new start of round.

Round 10: *(LT) twice, (RT) twice, rep from * to end.
Round 11: Knit.
Round 12: *K1, (LT) twice, RT, k1, rep from * to end.
Round 13: Knit.
Round 14: *K2, (LT) twice, k2, rep from * to end.
Round 15: Knit.
Round 16: *K1, RT, (LT) twice, k1, rep from * to end.
Rep rounds 1 through 16 three times more, then work rounds 1 through 11 once more.

HEEL
Note: The heel is worked flat over the first 32[32:40] sts, inc after row 1 to 34[34:42] sts.
Row 1: (RS) Sl1, m1, LT, k2, RT, k1, *k1, LT, k2, RT, k1, rep from * once[once:twice] more, k1, LT, k2, RT, m1, k1, turn (2 sts increased-34[34:42] sts).
Row 2: (WS): Sl1, *p1, k1, p4, k1, p1, rep from * 3[3:4] times more, p1.
Row 3: Sl1, *k1, p1, LT, RT, p1, k1, rep from * 3[3:4] times more, k1.
Row 4: Sl1, p1 *k2, p2, rep from * to end.
Row 5: Sl1, k1, *p2, k2, rep from * to end.
Rep rows 4 and 5 twelve times more for a total of 15 slipped sts on each side of heel flap.

Heel turn
Row 1: (WS) Sl1, p17[17:21], p2tog, p1, turn.
Row 2: (RS): Sl1, k3, ssk, k1, turn.
Row 3: Sl1, p4 (purling to one st before gap), p2tog, p1, turn.
Row 4: Sl1, k5 (knitting to one st before gap), ssk, k1, turn.
Cont in this manner until 20[20:24] sts rem.
Next row: (WS) Sl1, p16[16:20], p2tog, turn.
Next row: (RS) Sl1, k16[16:20], ssk. Do not turn (18[18:22] sts).

GUSSET

Round 1: Pick up and k1 st in each of the 16 slipped sts down the side of the heel flap, pm, work row 1 of Instep Chart on held 32[40:40] instep sts, pm, pick up and k1 st in each of the 16 slipped sts down the side of the heel flap, k9[9:11]. This is the new start of round (82[90:94] sts).

Round 2: K9[9:11], k15tbl, sl1, remove marker, slip st back to left needle, pm, k2tog, k to within 1 st of marker, ssk (removing marker), pm, k15tbl, k to end.

Round 3: K to marker, work next row of Instep Chart to marker, k to end.

Round 4: K to within 1 st of marker, sl1, remove marker, slip st back to left needle, pm, k2tog, k to within 1 st of marker, ssk (removing marker), pm, k to end.

Rep rounds 3 and 4 until 28[30:40] sole sts rem (60[70:80] sts).

FOOT

Cont working Instep Chart over 32[40:40] instep sts until foot measures 2 ½[3:3]in (6.5[7.5:7.5]cm) less than desired finished measurement, ending with round 8 or 16.

TOE
Set-up

K to marker. This is new start of round.

If you ended with Round 8

Round 1: K1, RT, k2, LT, *k2, RT, k2, LT, rep from * to last st before marker, k1, sm, k to end.

Small and medium sizes only

Round 2: K2tog, k to within 2 sts of marker, ssk, sl marker, k to end (30[38] instep sts, 28[30] sole sts).

Round 3: K5, *LT, RT, k4, rep from * to last st before marker, k1, sm, k to end.

Round 4: Ssk, k to within 2 sts of marker, k2tog, sm, k to end (28[36] instep sts, 28[30] sole sts).

Round 5: Knit.

Medium size only

Rep rounds 4 and 5 three times more (30 instep sts).

Large size only

Round 2: K2tog, k to within 2 sts of marker, ssk, sl marker, ssk, k to last 2 sts, k2tog (38 instep sts, 38 sole sts).

Round 3: K5, *LT, RT, k4, rep from * to within 1 st of marker, k1, sm, k to end.

If you ended with Round 16

Round 1: K1, LT, k2, RT, *k2, LT, k2, RT, rep from * to within 1 st of marker, k1, sm, k to end.

Small and medium sizes only

Round 2: K2tog, k to within 2 sts of marker, ssk, sm, k to end (30[38] instep sts, 28[30] sole sts).

Round 3: K1, LT, RT, *k4, LT, RT, rep from * to within 1 st of marker, k1, sm, k to end.

Round 4: K2tog, k to within 2 sts of marker, ssk, sm, k to end (28[36] instep sts, 28[30] sole sts).

Round 5: Knit.

Medium size only

Round 6: Ssk, k to within 2 sts of marker, k2tog, sm, k to end (34 instep sts, 30 sole sts).

Round 7: Knit.

Rep rounds 6 and 7 twice more (30 instep sts, 30 sole sts).

Large size only

Round 2: K2tog, k to within 2 sts of marker, ssk, sm, ssk, k to last 2 sts, k2tog (38 instep sts, 38 sole sts).

Round 3: K1, LT, RT, *k4, LT, RT, rep from * to within 1 st of marker, k1, sm, k to end.

Toe shaping
All sizes

Round 1: Ssk, k to within 2 sts of marker, k2tog, sm, ssk, k to last 2 sts, k2tog.

Round 2: Knit.

Rep rounds 1 and 2 until 40 sts rem.

Rep round 1 only until 16 sts rem.

FINISHING

Cut yarn, leaving an 8in (20cm) tail. With tail threaded on a tapestry needle, graft toe shut. Weave in ends.

Instep Chart

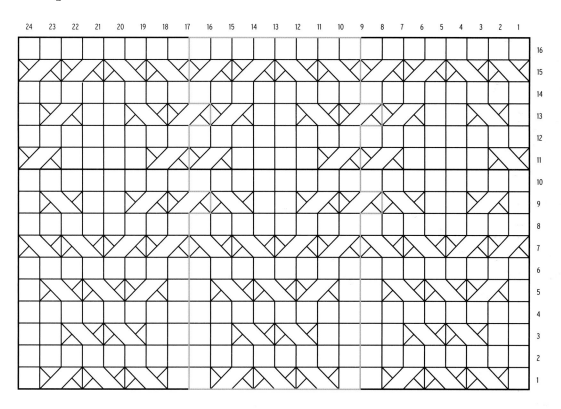

Shur'tugal

These socks were designed for my father-in-law, Frank, and named after the dragon riders in Christopher Paolini's *Inheritance Cycle* novels. They're meant to be worn by Shur'tugals to keep their feet protected and toasty warm during long flights with their dragons.

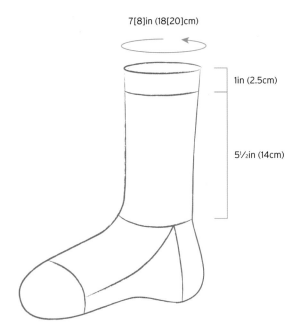

7[8]in (18[20]cm)

1in (2.5cm)

5½in (14cm)

SOCK VITALS

Yarn
Sokkusu Original 100% superwash merino
(433yds/396m per 120g):
1 skein in Draken

Needles
US 1.5 (2.5mm) or size needed to obtain
correct gauge

Gauge
36 sts to 4in (10cm) in stockinette stitch

Notions
Stitch markers
Tapestry needle

Technique notes

Doubled-tail long-tail cast on: Double
the length of the tail and fold it in half;
treat the doubled strand as the tail and
cast on using long tail method as usual.
This gives you greater elasticity and also
a nice rolled edge.
RT (right twist): See Farmer McGregor
page 62.
LT (left twist): See Farmer McGregor
page 62.

CUFF
Cast on 64[72] sts using doubled-tail long-tail
cast on. Join to work in the round, being careful
not to twist sts. Pm to mark beg of round.
Round 1: K1, (p2, k2) until 3 sts rem, p2, k1.
Rep round 1 until rib measures 1in (2.5cm).

LEG

Following the Leg Chart or written rounds, rep rounds 1 through 12 until the work measures approximately 6in (15cm) from cast-on edge, ending with round 12.

Leg pattern

Round 1: *K1, p2, k2, p2, k1, rep from * 7[8] times more.

Round 2: *K1, p1, RT, LT, p1, k1, rep from * 7[8] times more.

Round 3: *K1, p1, k1, p2, k1, p1, k1, rep from * 7[8] times more.

Round 4: *K1, RT, p2, LT, k1, rep from * 7[8] times more.

Round 5: *K2, p4, k2, rep from * 7[8] times more.

Round 6: Knit.

Round 7: *K1, p2, k2, p2, k1, rep from * 7[8] times more.

Round 8: *LT, p1, k2, p1, RT, rep from * 7[8] times more.

Round 9: *P1, k1, p1, k2, p1, k1, p1, rep from * 7[8] times more.

Round 10: *P1, LT, k2, RT, p1, rep from * 7[8] times more.

Round 11: *P2, k4, p2, rep from * 7[8] times more.

Round 12: Knit.

HEEL

Following the Heel Chart or written rounds, work the first 32 (sole) sts in rounds 1 through 4 in Heel Pattern and the remaining 32[40] (instep) sts in rounds 1 through 4 in Leg Pattern as established.

Heel pattern

Round 1: *K1, p2, k2, p2, k1, rep from * 3 times more.

Round 2: *K1, p1, RT, LT, p1, k1, rep from * 3 times more.

Round 3: *K1, p1, k4, p1, k1, rep from * 3 times more.

Round 4: *K1, RT, k2, LT, k1, rep from * 3 times more.

Heel flap

At this point, the sole sts are worked back and forth in rows and the 32[40] instep sts remain unworked.

Row 1: (RS) M1, k32, m1 (34 sole sts).

Row 2: (WS) Sl2 wyif, *p6, sl2 wyif, rep from * 3 times more.

Row 3: Knit.

Rep rows 2 and 3 fourteen times more. There will be 15 slipped sts along each side edge of the heel flap.

Heel turn

Row 1: (WS) Sl 1, p17, p2tog, p1, turn.

Row 2: (RS) Sl1, k3, ssk, k1, turn.

Row 3: Sl1, p to 1 st before gap formed on previous row, p2tog (1 st from each side of gap), p1, turn.

Row 4: Sl1, k to 1 st before gap formed on previous row, ssk (1 st from each side of gap), k1, turn.

Rep rows 3 and 4 until 3 sts rem at either end on the outside edge of gap (22 sts).

Next row: (WS) Sl1, p to 1 st before gap formed on previous row, p2tog (1 st from each side of gap), p2tog, turn (20 sts).

Next row: Sl1, k to 1 st before gap formed on previous row, ssk (1 st from each side of gap), ssk. Do not turn (18 sts).

GUSSET

Pick-up round: Pick up and k15 sts up right side of the heel flap, pm, work 32[40] instep sts in patt as set, pm, pick up and k15 sts down left side of the heel flap, k18 heel sts, k15 to marker (80[88] sts with 32[40] instep sts and 48 sole sts).

Round 1: Sm, work instep sts in patt as set, sm, k sole sts to marker.

Round 2: (dec round) Sm, work instep sts in patt as set, sm, ssk, k to 2 sts before marker, k2tog.

Rep rounds 1 and 2 until 32 sole sts rem (64[72] sts).

FOOT

Continue working instep sts in patt as set and St st over sole sts until foot is 2in (5cm) less than desired finished length, ending with round 5 of Leg Pattern.

TOE SET-UP

Following the Toe Chart or written rounds, work 7 rounds to set up for the decreases.

Round 1: Sm, k sole sts to marker, sm, k instep sts to marker.

Round 2: Sm, k sole sts to marker, sm, *k1, p2, k2, p2, k1, rep from * 3[4] times more.

Round 3: Sm, k sole sts to marker, sm, *LT, p1, k2, p1, RT, rep from * 3[4] times more.

Round 4: Sm, k sole sts to marker, sm, *k2, p1, k2, p1, k2, rep from * 3[4] times more.

Round 5: Sm, k sole sts to marker, sm, *k1, LT, k2, RT, k1, rep from * 3[4] times more.

Round 6: Sm, k sole sts to marker, sm, k instep sts to m.

Round 7: Sm, k sole sts to marker, sm, *k2, LT, RT, k2, rep from * 3[4] times more.

Large size only

K2, LT, RT, ending with last 2 instep sts unworked. Move first and last 2 instep sts to needle holding sole sts; there are 36 sts each for the sole and instep. Move markers so they are between sole sts and instep sts.

TOE

Round 1: (dec round) *Sm, ssk, k to within 2 sts of marker, k2tog, rep from * once more (4 sts decreased).

Round 2: Knit.

Rep rounds 1 and 2, dec 4 sts every other round until 28 sts rem (14 sts each for sole and instep), then rep round 1 only until 16 sts rem.

FINISHING

Cut yarn, leaving an 8in (20cm) tail. With tail threaded on a tapestry needle, graft toe shut. Weave in ends.

CHART KEY

□ knit

◿◺ LT

◺◿ RT

● purl

Leg Chart

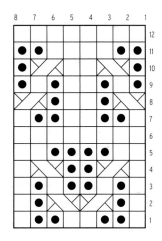

Heel Chart

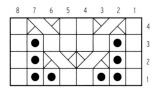

Toe Chart

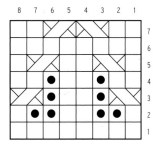

2luvcrew

Co-organizing Knit Nation with Cookie A is a big job
and one that can't be done without a lot of helping hands.
This sock, with all its asymmetric lace hearts, is dedicated
to the Knit Nation crew of volunteers who help to make
the event so successful and so much fun.

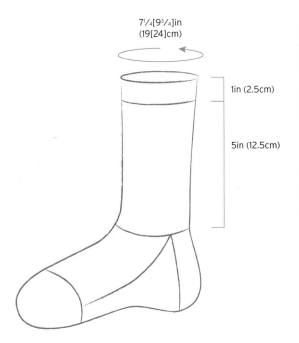

7¼[9¾]in
(19[24]cm)

1in (2.5cm)

5in (12.5cm)

SOCK VITALS

Yarn
Sokkusu Lightweight 100% superwash merino
(472yds/432m per 100g):
1 skein in Vamp Juice

Needles
US 1.5 (2.5mm) or size needed to obtain
correct gauge

Gauge
36 sts to 4in (10cm) in stockinette stitch

Notions
Stitch markers
Tapestry needle

Technique note

Channel Island cast on
Start in the same way as a long-tail
cast on. **1**
Wrap tail end around thumb counter-
clockwise twice. **2**
Insert needle under both strands on the
thumb. **3**
Using strand around finger, create a yarn
over. **4**
Pull yarn over back through both strands
on thumb. **5**
Pull out any slack from both ends of
yarn. **6**
Yarn over. **7**
Repeat steps 1-7. **8**

CUFF
Cast on 66[88] sts using a Channel Island cast
on. Join to work in the round being careful not
to twist sts.
Round 1: *P1, k1tbl, rep from * to end.
Rep round 1 until rib measures 1in (2.5cm).

LEG
Rounds 1-5: Work rows 1 to 5 of Cuff Transition
Chart.
Rounds 6-15: Work rows 1 to 10 of Heart
Pattern Chart.
Rep rounds 6 through 15 four times more, then
work rounds 6 to 10 once more (corresponding
to rows 1 through 5 of Heart Pattern Chart).

Channel Island cast on

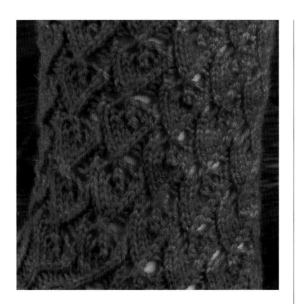

HEEL

Over the first 25[36] sts work row 1 of Heel Transition Chart 2[3] times, then work columns 1 through 3 once more, and pm (23[33] sts). Continue working row 6 of Heart Pattern Chart as set to end of round.
Work rows 2 through 6 of Heel Transition Chart as set to m, sm, and cont working Heart Pattern Chart as set to end of round (Rows 7 through 10, then row 1 once more).

Heel flap

The heel is now worked flat. On RS rows slip the first st purlwise with yarn in front, bring to back then work the next st as set. On WS rows slip the first st purlwise with the yarn in back.
Row 1: (RS) Sl1, work ribbing as set in row 7 of Heel Transition Chart to m, p1, turn (29[39] heel sts).
Row 2: (WS) Sl1, continue working ribbing as set by row 1.
Continue the ribbing as set until you have 15 slipped sts down each side.

Heel turn

Row 1: (WS) Sl1, p15[17], p2tog, p1, turn.
Row 2: Sl1, k4, ssk, k1, turn.
Row 3: Sl1, p5 (to 1 st before gap), p2tog, p1, turn.
Row 4: Sl1, k6 (to 1 st before gap), ssk, k1, turn.
Cont in this manner until 17[19] sts rem, ending with a RS row. Do not turn.

GUSSET SHAPING

Round 1: Pick up and k1 st in each of the 15 slipped sts down the side of the heel flap, pm, work row 2 of Instep Chart on instep sts, pm, pick up and k1 st in each of the 15 slipped sts up the side of the heel flap, k to end.

Note: From this point forward, the first and last st of the instep sts on every alt row will be decreased until 29[39] heel sts rem. You will need to move the markers to accommodate the decreases. The sts between the markers are the instep sts. The sts before the first marker and after the second marker are the sole sts.

Round 2: K14tbl, k2tog (removing marker), move previous st back to left needle, pm, sl1, work in patt to last instep st, ssk (removing m), pm, k14tbl, k to end.
Round 3: K to marker, sm, work instep sts in patt as set, sm, k to end.
Round 4: K to within 1 st of m, k2tog (removing marker), move st back to left needle, pm, sl1, work in patt to last instep st, ssk (removing marker), pm, k to end.
Note: When you come to the instep decreases at the end of rows 6, 8, and 10 of the Instep Chart, make a central decrease by slipping 2 sts tog as if to knit, then slipping 1 more st knitwise and knitting these 3 sts tog tbl.
Rep rounds 3 and 4 until 29[39] sole sts rem.

FOOT

Set up: K to marker and remove it. New start of round.

Round 1: Work instep sts in patt as set, sm, k to end. Cont working patt as set on instep sts and knitting sole sts until foot measures 2.5in (6.5cm) less than desired finished length, ending with row 10 of the Heart Pattern Chart.

TOE

Rounds 1–7: Work rows 1 through 7 of Toe Chart to m, k to end of round.

Cont working row 7 of Toe Chart to m, k to end of round, and at the same time on every alt round, work an ssk at the start of the round and a k2tog before the marker until there are 29[39] sts before the marker (58[78] sts).

Decrease rounds

Round 1: Ssk, work toe ribbing to 2 sts before marker, k2tog, sm, ssk, k to last 2 sts, k2tog (4 sts decreased).

Round 2: Work even in patts as set.

Rep rounds 1 and 2, working toe ribbing over instep sts, until 38 sts rem, then rep round 1 only until 6 sts rem.

FINISHING

Cut yarn, leaving an 8in (20cm) tail. With tail threaded on a tapestry needle, graft toe shut. Weave in ends.

Cuff Transition Chart

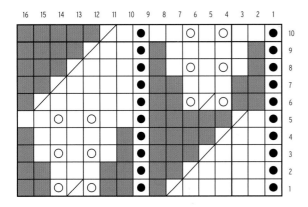

Heart Pattern Chart

Heel Transition Chart

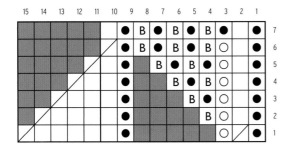

Instep Chart

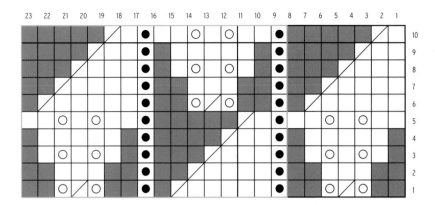

Toe Chart

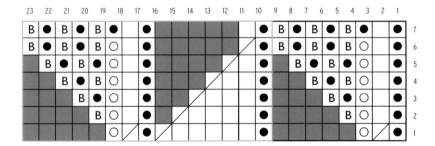

CHART KEY

B	knit tbl	⟋ (slash)	ssk
	knit	(gray)	no stitch
⟋	k2tog	○	yo
●	purl		pattern repeat

Vorticity

Water can be as mesmerising as fire—the swirls, eddies and vortices, the ripples and waves. It's constantly changing, like the swirl pattern on this sock which gently shifts as you knit it. Use a subtle, variegated yarn or a semi solid yarn to bring out the elegant rivulets which sashay down the sock.

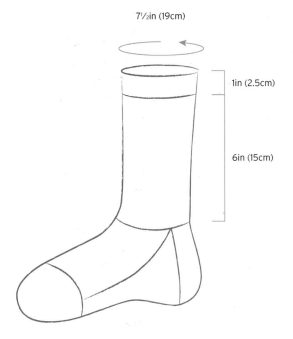

7½in (19cm)

1in (2.5cm)

6in (15cm)

SOCK VITALS

Yarn
Sokkusu Original 100% superwash merino
(433yds/396m per 120g):
1 skein in Swansong

Needles
US 1.5 (2mm) or size needed to obtain
correct gauge

Gauge
36 sts to 4in (10cm) in stockinette stitch

Notions
Stitch markers
Tapestry needle

CUFF
Cast on 70 sts. Join to work in the round being
careful not to twist sts.
Round 1: K2, p2, k2, p2, *k4, p2, k2, p2, rep
from * to last 2 sts, k2.
Rep round 1 until rib measures 1in (2.5cm).

LEG
Round 1: Work row 1 of Leg Chart (77sts).
Round 2: Work row 2 of Leg Chart (70 sts).
Rounds 3-21: Continue working Leg Chart
as set.
Rep Rounds 1 through 21 twice more.
Rep Rounds 1 through 19 once more.

HEEL
Heel set-up: K4. New start of round.
The heel is worked flat on 30 sts; place rem sts
on hold for instep.
Row 1: (RS) K30, turn.
Row 2: Sl1, p to end.
Row 3: *Sl1, k1, rep from * to end.
Rep rows 2 and 3 fourteen times more.

Heel turn
Row 1: Sl1, p16, p2tog, p1, turn.
Row 2: Sl1, k5, ssk, k1, turn.
Row 3: Sl1, p6 (to one stitch before gap), p2tog,
p1, turn.
Row 4: Sl1, k7 (to one stitch before gap), ssk,
k1, turn.
Continue in this manner until all heel sts have
been worked and 18 sts rem, ending with a RS
row. Do not turn.

GUSSET SHAPING
Set-up round: Pick up and k1 st in each of the
15 slipped sts down the side of the heel flap, k1.
New start of round.

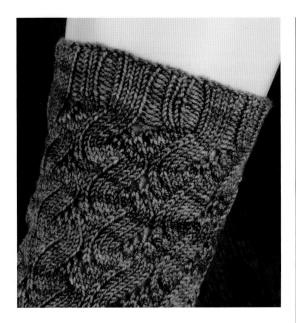

Round 1: K38 instep stitches, pm, K1, pick up and k1 st in each of the 15 slipped sts up the side of the heel flap, K18, k15tbl, k1.

Note: The sts before the marker are the instep sts. They vary in stitch count depending on the chart row. The sts after the marker to the end of round are the sole stitches. You will dec every other round at both ends of the sole stitches.

Round 2: K38, sm, ssk, k14tbl, k to last 2 sts, k2tog.
Round 3: Work row 1 of Instep Chart, sm, k to end of round.
Round 4: Work row 2 of chart, sm, ssk, k to last 2 sts, k2tog.
Continue as set in rounds 3 and 4, working the chart over the instep sts, and dec 2 sts every alt round on the sole stitches until 32 sole sts rem.

FOOT

Continue in patt over instep sts and work St st over sole stitches until foot measures 3in (7.5cm) less than desired finished length, ending with any even numbered row of the chart except row 2, 4, or 6.

TOE

Round 1: K1, ssk, k to within 3 sts of marker, k2tog, k1, sm, k to end of round.
Round 2: Knit.
Rounds 3-6: Rep rounds 1 and 2 twice more (32 instep sts and 32 sole sts).
Round 7: *K1, ssk, k to within 3 sts of marker, k2tog, k1, sm, rep from * to end of round.
Round 8: Knit.
Rep rounds 3 and 4 until 28 sts rem (14 instep and 14 sole sts).
Rep round 3 only until 12 sts rem (6 instep and 6 sole sts).

FINISHING

Cut yarn, leaving an 8in (20cm) tail. With tail threaded on a tapestry needle, graft toe shut. Weave in ends.

Leg Chart

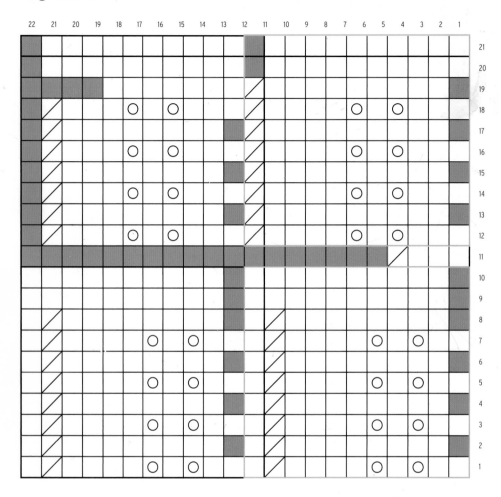

CHART KEY

☐	knit	▨	no stitch
◩	k2tog	⊡	yo
☐	new start of round	☐	pattern repeat

Instep Chart

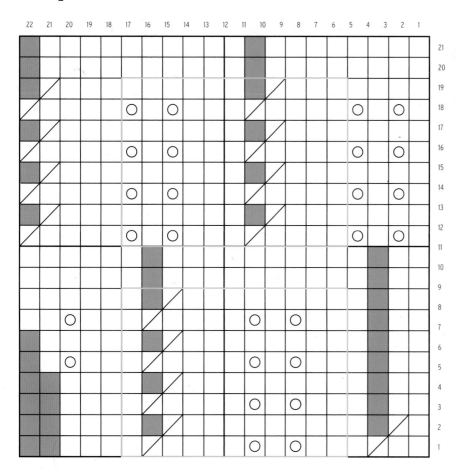

Rumpled!

The first sock of my 2010 Knit Love Club, this was an instant hit. I love the elegant stitch pattern and the lovely textured fabric it creates that looks like a wheatsheaf. The name for the sock is a word play on Rumpelstiltskin, the guy who helped a farm girl spin wheat into gold in exchange for her first born, but who in his hubris, got rumbled in the end.

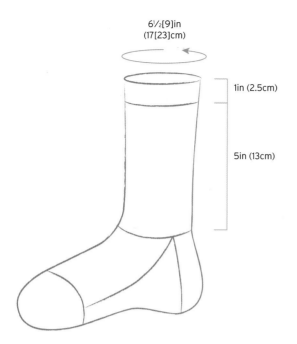

6½[9]in
(17[23]cm)

1in (2.5cm)

5in (13cm)

SOCK VITALS

Yarn
Sokkusu Original 100% superwash merino
(433yds/396m per 120g):
1 skein in Tangerina

Needles
For small size: US 1 (2.25mm) or size needed
to obtain correct gauge
For medium and large sizes: US 1.5 (2.5mm)
or size needed to obtain correct gauge

Gauge
For small size: 44 sts to 4in (10cm) over
stockinette stitch using size 1 needles

For medium and large sizes: 36 sts to 4in
(10cm) over stockinette stitch using size
1.5 needles

Notions
Stitch markers
Tapestry needle

CUFF
Cast on 72 sts. Join to work in the round being
careful not to twist sts.
Round 1: (P1, k1tbl) to end.
Rep round 1 until twisted rib measures 1in (2.5cm).

LEG
Work rows 1-24 of Rumple Stitch Chart twice,
then work rows 1-9 once more.
P1. This is now the new start of round.

Knit 4 stitches together

Slip 4 stitches together

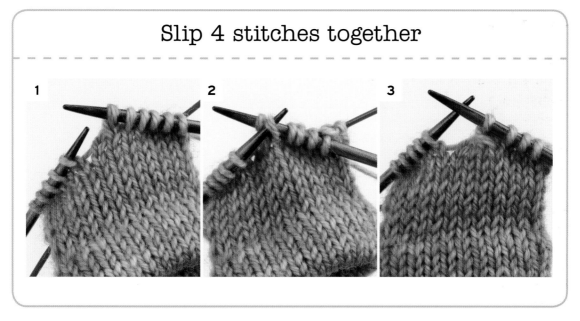

HEEL

Divide for heel flap

Set-up row (RS): M1, (sl1, k1) 17 times, sl1, m1. Place rem 37 sts on hold for the instep. Turn work so the wrong side is facing.

Row 1: (WS) Sl1, p36, turn.

Row 2: (RS) Sl1, *sl1, k1, rep from * to end.

Rep rows 1 and 2 seventeen times more.

Heel turn

Work back and forth in short rows to shape heel.

Row 1: (WS) Sl1, p20, p2tog, p1, turn.

Row 2: (RS) Sl1, k6, ssk, k1, turn.

Row 3: (WS) Sl1, p7, p2tog, p1, turn.

Row 4: (RS) Sl1, k8, ssk, k1, turn.

Cont working short rows as set by rows 3 and 4, working 1 st more before the decrease every row (so on row 5 you would sl1, p9, p2tog, p1 turn, and then row 6 you would sl1, k10, ssk, k1, turn, etc.) until all sts have been worked and ending with a RS row (21 heel sts rem). Do not turn.

SHAPE GUSSET

With RS facing, pick up and k17 sts (1 for every slipped st) down the side of the heel flap, pm, work the held instep sts in patt, pm, pick up and k17 sts (1 for every slipped st) up the other side of the heel flap, pm or divide sts accordingly to mark new start of round.

Note: There are 37 sts in the instep section, so you will be working the Rumple Stitch Chart twice, then the first stitch of the chart once more.

Round 1: K to within 2 sts of marker, k2tog, work instep sts in Rumple Stitch as set to marker, ssk, k to end of round (2 sts decreased).

Round 2: K to marker, work Rumple Stitch to marker, k to end of round.

Note: You may find knitting tbl of the previous ssk st helps straighten the decrease line.

Rep rounds 1 and 2 until 35(31:35) heel sts rem (72[68:72] sts).

FOOT

Set up row: K to marker, work Rumple Stitch to marker. This is the new start of round. Knit to marker, then work Rumple Stitch to marker as set without further sole decreases, until foot measures approximately 2in (5cm) less than desired finished length from back of heel, ending with row 13, 17, or 21 of Rumple Stitch Chart.

TOE

Round 1: K to marker, *k1tbl, p1, rep from * to last st, k1tbl.

Round 2: K to marker, ssk, *k1tbl, p1, rep from * to last 3 sts, k1tbl, k2tog (2 sts decreased). (35 instep sts, 35[31:35] sole sts).

Medium size only

Cont twisted rib on the instep sts at the same time dec 2 sts on every alt round on the instep sts only until 31 instep sts and 31 sole sts rem.

All sizes

Round 3: K to marker, k1, *k1tbl, p1, rep from * to last st, k1.

Round 4: Ssk, k to within 2 sts of marker, k2tog, sm, ssk, *k1tbl, p1, rep from * to last 2 sts, k2tog. Rep rounds 3 and 4 until 34 sts rem, then rep round 4 only until 14 sts rem.

FINISHING

Cut yarn, leaving an 8in (20cm) tail. With tail threaded on a tapestry needle, graft toe shut. Weave in ends.

Rumple Stitch Chart

18	17	16	15	14	13	12	11	10	9	8	7	6	5	4	3	2	1	
						●	B	●	B	●								24
						●	B	●	B	●								23
						●	B	●	B	●								22
O		O		O	k4tog	●	B	●	B	●	s4k	O		O		O		21
						●	B	●	B	●								20
						●	B	●	B	●								19
						●	B	●	B	●								18
O		O		O	k4tog	●	B	●	B	●	s4k	O		O		O		17
						●	B	●	B	●								16
						●	B	●	B	●								15
						●	B	●	B	●								14
O		O		O	k4tog	●	B	●	B	●	s4k	O		O		O		13
B	●													●	B	●		12
B	●													●	B	●		11
B	●													●	B	●		10
B	●	k4tog	O		O		O		O		O	s4k		●	B	●		9
B	●													●	B	●		8
B	●													●	B	●		7
B	●													●	B	●		6
B	●	k4tog	O		O		O		O		O	s4k		●	B	●		5
B	●													●	B	●		4
B	●													●	B	●		3
B	●													●	B	●		2
B	●	k4tog	O		O		O		O		O	s4k		●	B	●		1

CHART KEY

☐ knit	◻ (diagonal) ssk
◻ (diagonal) k2tog	B tbl
● purl	O yo
◹ k4tog	
◺ s4k	

Crowley

I'm a big fan of the TV series *Supernatural*, and this
sock is named after Crowley, the King of the Crossroads.
Crossing cables run the length of the leg and then
melt into ribbing for the foot.

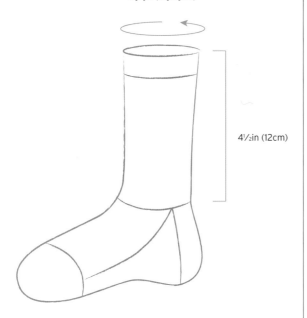

6[7]in (15[18]cm)

4½in (12cm)

SOCK VITALS

Yarn

Sokkusu Xtra 70% merino 20% cashmere 10% nylon (400yds/366m per 113g):
1 skein in Devilsnare

Needles

US 2 (2.75mm) or size needed to obtain correct gauge

Gauge

36 sts to 4in (10cm) in stockinette stitch

Notions

Stitch markers
Cable needle
Tapestry needle

Technique notes

C6L: Slip 4 sts to cable needle (cn) and hold in front, k2 from left needle, slip 2 from cn to left needle, k2 from left needle, k2 from cn.
C6R: Slip 4 sts to cn and hold in back, k2 from left needle, slip 2 from cn to left needle, k2 from left needle, k2 from cn.
C5L: Slip 3 sts to cn and hold in front, k2 from left needle, slip 1 from cn to left needle, k1 from left needle, k2 from cn.
C5R: Slip 3 sts to cn and hold in back, k2 from left needle, slip 1 from cn to left needle, k1 from left needle, k2 from cn.

LEG

Cast on 60[72] sts. Join to work in the round being careful not to twist sts.
Note: The start of the round shifts by 2[3] sts on round 19 and then is restored by 2[3] sts on round 22.
Rounds 1-18: Work Crossroads Chart 6 times each round (60[72] sts).
Round 19: Work Crossroads Chart 6 times, k2[3] (62[75] sts worked). This is the new start of round.
Rounds 20 to 21: Work Crossroads Chart 6 times each round (60[72] sts).
Round 22: Work Crossroads Chart 5 times, p2, k1[2], p2, k3 (58[69] sts). This is the new start of round (restored to original start).
Rounds 23 to 24: Work Crossroads Chart 6 times each round (60[72] sts).
Rep rounds 1 through 24 once more, then work rounds 1 through 12 once more.

HEEL

The heel is worked flat over the first 29[36] sts. The rem 31[36] sts are the held instep sts.

Row 1: (RS) M0[1], *k0[1], p1, k2, p1, k1[2], p1, k2, p1, k1, rep from * once more, then k0[1], p1, k2, p1, k1[2], p1, k2, p1, k0[1], m0[1] (29[38]sts).

Row 2: (WS) Sl1, then p the k sts and k the p sts from the previous row.

Row 3: Sl1, *k0[1], p0[1], k2, p1, k1[2], p1, k2, p1, k1, p1[0], rep from * once more, then k0[1], p0[1], k2, p1, k1[2], p1, k2, p1, k0[2].

Rep rows 2 and 3 fourteen more times for a total of 15 slipped sts on each side of the heel flap.

Heel turn

Row 1: (WS) Sl1, p15[20], p2tog, p1, turn.
Row 2: (RS) Sl1, k4[5], ssk, k1, turn.
Row 3: Sl1, p5[6], (1 st before gap), p2tog, p1, turn.
Row 4: Sl1, k6[7], (1 st before gap), ssk, k1, turn.
Continue in this manner until 17[26] sts rem ending with RS row.

Small size only
Do not turn.

Large size only
Row 1: Sl1, p18, p2tog, p2tog, turn.
Row 2: Sl1, k19, ssk, ssk (22 sts). Do not turn.

GUSSET

Round 1: Pick up 1 st in each of the 15 slipped sts down the side of the heel flap, k1 from the held instep sts, pm.

Small size only
Gusset Rib: *P1, k2, p1, k1, p1, k2, p1, k1, rep from * once more, p1, k2, p1, k1, p1, k2, p1, pm, k1.

Large size only
Gusset Rib: P1, *k2, p1, rep from * 11 times to one st from end of instep, pm, k1.

All sizes
Pick up 1 st in each of the 15 slipped sts up the side of the heel flap, k to end. The sts between the markers are the instep sts. The sts before the first marker and after the second marker are the sole sts.

Round 2: K to within 2 sts of marker (k picked up sts tbl), k2tog, sm, work instep according to the rib pattern as set in round 1 to marker, sm, ssk, k to end.

Round 3: K to marker, cont working instep as set, sm, k to end.

Cont repeating rounds 2 and 3 until 60[72] sts rem.

FOOT
Small size only
K to 1 st before marker. This is the new start of round.

Foot Rib: K1, remove marker, *p1, k2, p1, k1, p1, k2, p1, k1, rep from * once more, p1, k2, p1, k1, p1, k2, p1, remove marker, k1, pm, k to end (31 instep sts, 29 sole sts).

Large size only
Continue working instep as set from Gusset section and sole in St st.

All sizes
Cont working Foot Rib as set until foot measures 1½[2]in (4[5]cm) less than desired finished length.

TOE
Small size only
Set-up round: P2tog, work Foot Rib as set until 2 sts before marker, ssp, k to end (29 instep sts, 29 sole sts).

Round 1: Work Foot Rib as set to marker (do not work decreased sts at beg and end of instep), k to end.

Round 2: P1, k1, ssk, work rem instep as set to 4

sts before marker, k2tog, k1, p1, sm, p1, k1, ssk, k to 4 sts before end, k2tog, k1, p1 (54 sts).

Round 3: P1, k2, work Foot Rib as set to 3 sts before marker, k2, p1, k to end.

Round 4: P1, k1, ssk, work rem instep as set to 4 sts before marker, k2tog, k1, p1, sm, p1, k1, ssk, k to 4 sts before end, k2tog, k1, p1 (50 sts).
Rep rounds 3 and 4, dec 4 sts every alt round as set, until 38 sts rem.
Rep round 4 only until 18 sts rem.

Last round: K2tog, ssk, k1, k2tog, ssk, sm, k2tog, ssk, k1, k2tog, ssk.

Large size only
Set-up round: Work Foot Rib on instep to marker, k1, ssk, k to 3 sts before end, k2tog, k1 (34 instep sts, 36 sole sts).

Round 1: Work Foot Rib as set to marker, sm, k to end.

Round 2: Work Foot Rib on instep to marker, sm, k1, ssk, k to 3 sts before end, k2tog, k1 (34 instep sts, 34 sole sts).

Round 3: Work Foot Rib as set to marker, sm, k to end.

Round 4: Rep round 2 (34 instep sts, 32 sole sts).
Round 5: Rep round 3.
Round 6: P1, k1, ssk, work Foot Rib to 4 sts before marker, k2tog, k1, p1, sm, k1, ssk, k to 3 sts from end, k2tog, k1 (62 sts).
Rep rounds 5 and 6, dec 4 sts every alt round, until 38 sts rem.
Rep round 6 only until 14 sts rem.

Last round: K2tog, ssk, k2tog, ssk, sm, k1, ssk, ktog, k1.

FINISHING
Cut yarn, leaving an 8in (20cm) tail. With tail threaded on a tapestry needle, graft toe shut. Weave in ends.

Crossroads Chart

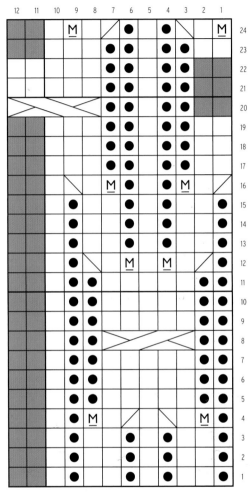

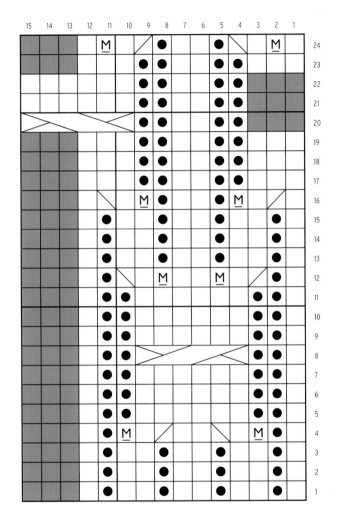

CHART KEY

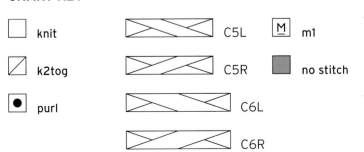

- ☐ knit
- ╱ k2tog
- ● purl
- ⤬ C5L
- ⤬ C5R
- ⤬ C6L
- ⤬ C6R
- Ⓜ m1
- ▨ no stitch

Om Shanti

When you need a little bit of pampering, a little shot
of cashmere and luxury, these socks are just the ticket.
Designed as bed socks, to be knit in a luxury yarn, these
socks sport a soft and cushy texture, and an unusual
corrugated ribbed cuff set off with an Estonian braid.
Cozy up in these socks with a book and cup of hot chocolate.

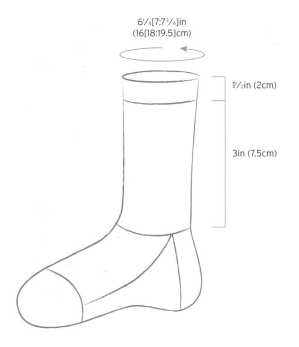

6¼[7:7¾]in
(16[18:19.5]cm)

1½in (2cm)

3in (7.5cm)

SOCK VITALS

Yarn

Sokkusu Xtra 70% merino 20% cashmere 10%
nylon (400yds/366m per 113g)
1 skein in Freshwater separated into 1 ball of
90% of the yarn and a smaller ball of 10% of
the yarn for the cuff

Needles

US 2 (2.75mm) or size needed to obtain
correct gauge

Gauge

32 sts to 4in (10cm) in stockinette stitch

Notions

Approx 48in (122cm) of contrast color waste yarn
4/E (3.5mm) crochet hook
Tapestry needle

Pattern notes

These socks are worked toe up using garter
stitch short rows for the toe and heel. The
stitches are wrapped but the wraps are left
in situ, blending in with the garter stitch.
The pattern stitch is an Estonian 3-cross lace
stitch, which decreases on the first round, then
increases back to the original stitch count in
the following round.

Note that the garter stitch heel is worked over
60% of the stitches, not the more common
50%. This results in less strain at the joining
points of the heel. You can work it over 60–
70% for a better fit if you have high arches.

The cuff uses another Estonian technique
called Kihnu Vits–it is a braid using 2 strands
of yarn worked with the purl stitch, carrying
both strands at the front of the work. The trick
is to make sure the working strand is always
brought up from under the previous working
strand. A 1 x 1 rib using both strands creates a
nice thick cuff to match the rest of the sock.
The finish is a very simple sewn bind off–the
Elizabeth Zimmerman Casting-on Casting-off
method–which is virtually indistinguishable
from a long-tail cast on.

TOE

With waste yarn, make a slipknot on your
crochet hook and then chain 25[27:29] sts
around your needle.
Set-up row: Move the crochet chain so that
the slipknot is nearest the tip of the left needle,
and the unraveling end is at the far left. Change
to working yarn and knit 1 row. Turn.
Row 1: (RS) K to last st, WT (see page 48).
Row 2: (WS) K to last st, WT.

Row 3: K to last unwrapped st, WT.

Rep row 3 until 7 unwrapped sts rem in the middle, with 9[10:11] wrapped sts on each side, ending with a WS row.

Row 4: (RS) K7 unwrapped sts, then k the first wrapped st, WT.

Row 5: K8, then k the first wrapped st, WT.

Row 6: K to double wrapped st, k the double wrapped st, WT.

Rep row 6 until 1 double wrapped st remains on each side of the needle, ending with a WS row.

Row 7: M1[0:1], k25[27:29], m1[0:1] (27[27:31] instep sts).

Unzip the provisional cast on, placing 25[27:29] sts onto second needle, m0[1:0], K25[27:29], m0[1:0] (25[29:29] sole sts).

FOOT

Work the following stitch pattern over instep and continue with St st over sole sts.

Round 1: *Sl1, k2, psso, k1, rep from * to last 3 sts, sl1, k2, psso.

Round 2: *K1, yo, k2, rep from * to last 2 sts, k1, yo, k1.

Round 3: Knit.

Round 4: K2, *sl1, k2, psso, k1, rep from * to last st, k1.

Round 5: K2, *k1, yo, k2, rep from * to last st, k1.

Round 6: Knit.

Rep rounds 1 through 6 until foot is 2in (5cm) less than desired finished length, ending on round 5. Knit the sole sts.

HEEL

Move 2 stitches from each side of the instep to join the heel stitches in the next round as follows:

Set-up round: K to last 2 sts of instep. This now marks the beginning of the heel stitches.

Row 1: (RS) K27[31:31] heel sts. Bring next 2 sts from instep to join the heel sts, k the first of these 2 sts, then WT (29[33:33] heel sts, 28[32:32] active sts, 1 wrapped).

Row 2 (WS): The heel is now worked flat on these 29[33:33] heel sts only. K to last st, WT.

Row 3: K to last unwrapped stitch, WT.

Rep row 3 until 7 unwrapped sts rem in the middle, with 11[13:13] wrapped sts on each side, ending with a WS row.

Row 4: (RS) K7 unwrapped sts, and then k the first wrapped st, WT.

Row 5: K8, then k the first wrapped st, WT.

Row 6: K to double wrapped st, k the double wrapped st, WT.

Rep row 6 until all wrapped sts have been worked and one double wrapped st remains on each side of the needle, ending with a WS row.

Row 7: K to 2 last sts and move these back across to join instep stitches. This is the new start of the round.

LEG

Round 1: *Sl1, k2, psso, k1, rep from * to end of round.

Round 2: *K1, yo, k2, rep from * to end of round.

Round 3: Knit.

Round 4: K2, *sl1, k2, psso, k1, rep from * to last 2 sts. Bring first st from the start of the round back so that 3 sts rem on needle, sl1, k2, psso. New start of round–start of round has shifted to the left by 1 st.

Round 5: K1, *k1, yo, k2, rep from * to last 2 sts, k1, yo, k1.

Round 6: Knit.

Round 7: K3, *sl1, k2, psso, k1, rep from * to one st before end of round. New start of round–start of round has shifted to the right by 1 st.

Round 8: Sl first 3 sts of the round to right needle. Sl first st (far right) over second and third sts. Place resulting 2 sts back onto left needle.

Start round: *K1, yo, k2, rep from * to end of round.

Round 9: Knit.

Rep rounds 4 through 9 five times more, or until you have .35oz (10g) of yarn left for the cuff ending with round 6 or 9.

CUFF

Wind rem yarn into two smaller balls of equal weight. The first ball will be referred to as A, the second as B.

Kihnu Vits braid

Bring A to front and drop. Purl with B, **1** leaving tail end of B hanging to the front of the work. Pick up A, bringing A over the tail end of B, then under working end of B. **2** Purl 1. **3** * Pick up B, bringing it under A, p1. Pick up A, bringing it under B, p1. Rep from * to last st. **4** Bring B to the back of the work. Using A, p1 and bring yarn to the back of the work. Pass this st back to the left needle, bring tail end of B back between the needles, and pass the stitch from the left needle back to the right needle.

Corrugated ribbing

Round 1: *K1 with B, p1 with A (carrying both yarns at the back), rep from * to end of round. Rep round 1 eight times more or until cuff is desired length.

Bind off

Cut A leaving a tail 4 times the circumference of your cuff.

Kihnu Vits braid

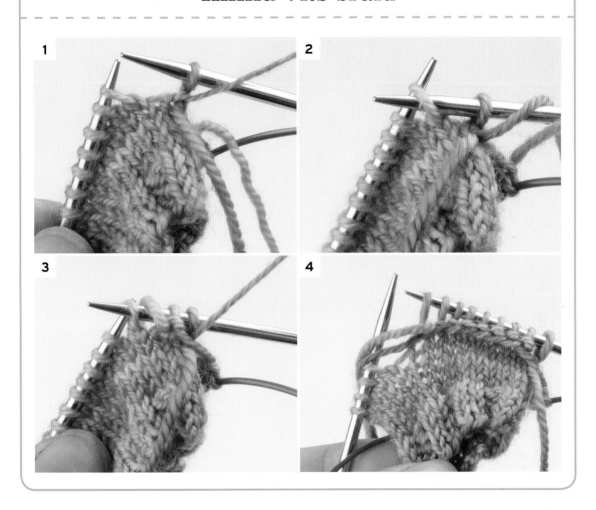

Working from left to right, using a blunt tapestry needle, and keeping the yarn above the sts, * insert needle into the second st from the front, and into the first st from the back. Pull the yarn through snugly. Drop the first st. Rep from * until all sts are bound off (see illustration opposite).

FINISHING

Weave in ends.

Elizabeth Zimmerman's sewn bind off

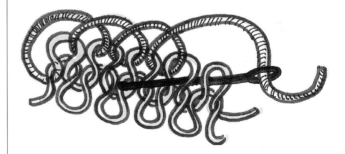

Mince Pie Mayhem

Lots of little cables create a lattice like the topping on mince pies, a surefire sign of the holidays in London. Knit up the socks, pop a couple of mince pies in the oven, and sit by a toasty fire, preferably with some mulled wine.

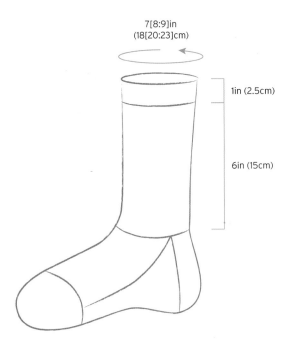

7[8:9]in
(18[20:23]cm)

1in (2.5cm)

6in (15cm)

Technique notes

m1L (make one left): Insert tip of right needle into the st below the first st on the left needle. Lift this st onto left needle without twisting and knit into this st.

m1R (make one right): Insert tip of left needle into the second st below the st on the right needle (i.e. not the st below the st just knitted, but the st below that). Lift this st onto left needle without twisting and knit into this st.

SOCK VITALS

Yarn
Sokkusu Original, 100% superwash merino (433yds/396m per 120g):
1 skein in Tree Frog

Needles
US 1.5 (2.5mm) or size needed to obtain correct gauge

Gauge
36 sts to 4in (10cm) over stockinette stitch

Notions
Stitch markers
Tapestry needle

CUFF
Cast on 72[80:88] sts. Join to work in the round being careful not to twist sts.
Round 1: (K2tbl, p2) to end.
Rep round 1 until rib measures 1in (2.5cm).

LEG
Begin Mince Pie Chart. **Note:** On round 3, k1 before beginning the chart row. This moves the start of this and rounds 4 through 8 by 1 st. At the end of round 8, work 1 fewer st at the end of the chart row, returning to the original start for round 1.

Work rounds 1 through 8 of Mince Pie Chart until leg is 5in (13cm) long, ending with round 8 and working the chart to the last st before the end of row. This is the new start for round 1 of the heel set-up.

HEEL
Heel set-up
Round 1: Work row 1 of Mince Pie Chart.

Small size only
Round 2: (WS) *K1tbl, m1L, m1R, k1tbl, p2, k2tbl, p2, (work row 2 of Mince Pie Chart) 3 times, k2tbl, p2, rep from * once more (76 sts).

Medium size only
Round 2: (WS) *K1tbl, m1L, m1R, k1tbl, p2, k2tbl, p2, (work row 2 of Mince Pie Chart) 4 times, rep from * once more (84 sts).

Large size only
Round 2: (WS) *K1tbl, m1L, m1R, k1tbl, p2, k2tbl, p2, (work row 2 of Mince Pie Chart) 4 times, k2tbl, p2, rep from * once more (92 sts).

All sizes
K2tbl, mark new start of round.

Heel expansion
The first 38[42:46] sts are the sole sts, the second 38[42:46] sts are the instep sts. You will inc 1 st at the beg and 1 st at the end of the sole sts only. The instep st count will remain 38[42:46].

Round 3: Work row 3 of Heel Expansion Chart over the sole sts (38[42:46] sts), then work row 3 of Heel Expansion Chart over the instep sts.

Round 4: M1, work row 4 of Heel Expansion Chart over the sole sts, m1 (40[44:48] sole sts), then work round 4 of Heel Expansion Chart over the instep sts.

Cont working Heel Expansion Chart as set over the instep sts. The following directions apply only to the sole sts.

Round 5: K1tbl, work row 5 of Heel Expansion Chart, k1tbl.

Round 6: M1, k1tbl, work row 6 of Heel Expansion Chart, k1tbl, m1 (42[46:50] sole sts).

Round 7: K2tbl, work row 7 of Heel Expansion Chart, k2tbl.

Round 8: M1, K2tbl, work row 8 of Heel Expansion Chart, k2tbl, m1 (44[48:52] sole sts).

Cont as set, inc 1 st at the beg and 1 st at the end of every even numbered row of Heel Expansion Chart on the sole sts only, until you have inc 11 sts each side of the sole sts (not including the set-up row increases), ending with row 1 of Heel Expansion Chart (60[64:68] sole sts, 38[42:46] instep sts).

Heel turn
Note: The heel turn is worked back and forth on the sole sts.

Row 1: K32[34:36], ssk, k1, turn (59[63:67] sts).
Row 2: Sl1, p5, p2tog, p1, turn (58[62:66] sts).
Row 3: Sl1, k6, ssk, k1, turn (57[61:65] sts).

Row 4: Sl1, p7, p2tog, p1, turn (56[60:64] sts).
Row 5: Sl1, k8, ssk, k1, turn (55[59:63] sts).
Cont in this manner until 3 sts rem on either side of the gap, ending with (WS) slip 1, p27[29:31], p2tog, p1, turn.
Next round: (RS) Sl1, k28[30:32], ssk, k2 (35[37:39] sole sts), do not turn, work round 2 of Heel Expansion Chart over instep sts. Cont in rounds, working Heel Expansion Chart as set over the instep sts.
Next round: K2, k2tog, k to end of sole sts. (34[36:38] sole sts, 38[42:46] instep sts)

FOOT

Continue working instep sts as set and St st over sole sts until foot is 1½in (4cm) less than desired finished length, ending with round 1 or 5 of Heel Expansion Chart.

TOE

Round 1: Knit.
Round 2: *K12[13:14], PM, rep from * 5 times more.
Round 3: *K to within 2 sts of marker, k2tog, rep from * 5 times more.
Round 4: Knit.
Round 5: Knit.
Rep rounds 3 through 5 until 42 sts rem.
Rep rounds 3 and 4 until 24 sts rem.
Rep round 3 until 6 sts rem.

FINISHING

Cut yarn, leaving an 8in (20cm) tail. With tail threaded on a tapestry needle, graft toe shut. Weave in ends.

Mince Pie Chart

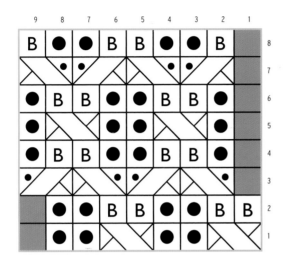

Heel Expansion Chart

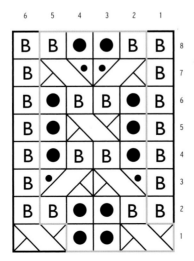

CHART KEY

B	knit tbl
●	purl
▦	no stitch
▢	pattern repeat
◺◹	left cable
◺◹•	left cable, purl
•◺◹	right cable, purl

Hundred Acre Wood

These socks were inspired by the TV series *Supernatural*.
The Winchester brothers are always bombing around
the forested backroads of America in their '67 Chevy
Impala. All the little leaves on this sock are an ode to
the eye candy in the show... Dean, Sam... the Impala.
Take your pick, they're all good.

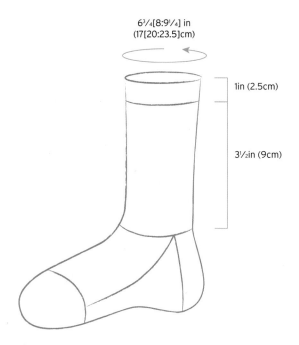

6¾[8:9¼] in
(17[20:23.5]cm)

1in (2.5cm)

3½in (9cm)

SOCK VITALS

Yarn
Sokkusu Original 100% superwash merino
(433yds/396m per 120g):
1 skein in Midnight Runner

Needles
US 1.5 (2.5mm) or size needed to obtain
correct gauge

Gauge
36 sts to 4in (10cm) in stockinette stitch

Notions
Stitch markers
Tapestry needle

Technique notes

mkfb (mirrored kfb): Slip next st knitwise,
slip back to left needle, and knit it knitwise.
Insert left needle tip into the st below the
st just made on right needle from front to
back (i.e. knitwise) and knit into this st.

ksw (knit shadow wrap) and **psw (purl
shadow wrap):** see Kwalla, pages 54 and 56.

TOE
Use the Turkish cast-on method as follows.
Leave a 5in (13cm) tail and bring yarn over two
needles held together with points to the right.
Wrap the working yarn around both needles 3
times, working from left to right and swinging
the yarn away from you and then back toward
you over the top of both needles. **1**
Set-up row: Using bottom needle if using
circulars, or third needle if using DPNs, **2** k3
from the top needle. **3**
Round 1: Holding tail and working yarn
together as a double strand, k6 (12 sts). Drop
the tail end. **4**
Round 2: With the working yarn only, k12, being
sure to knit each of the double strand sts (12
sts). **5**
Round 3: (K1, kfb) 6 times (18 sts).
Round 4: Knit.
Round 5: (K2, kfb) 6 times (24 sts).
Round 6: Knit.
Round 7: (K3, kfb) 6 times (30 sts).
Round 8: Knit.
Round 9: (K4, kfb) 6 times (36 sts).

Turkish cast on

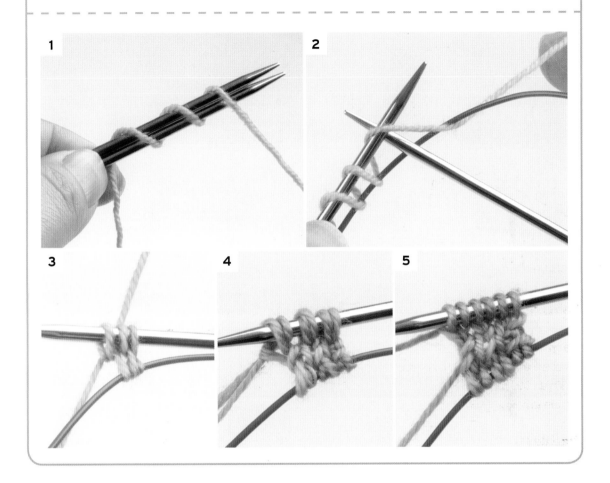

Round 10: (K6[5:5], p0[1:1]) 3 times, k to end of round.

Round 11: (K5, pfb0[1:1], kfb1[0:0]) 3 times, (k5, kfb) 3 times (42 sts).

Round 12: (K5, p0[1:2], k2[1:0]) 3 times, k to end of round.

Round 13: (K5, p0[1:1], k1[0:0], pfb0[0:1], kfb1[1:0]) 3 times, (k6, kfb) 3 times (48 sts).

Round 14: (K5, p0[1:2], k3[1:1], p0[1:0]) 3 times, k to end of round.

Round 15: (K5, p0[1:2], k2[1:0], pfb0[1:0], kfb1[0:1]) 3 times, (k7, kfb) 3 times (54 sts).

Round 16: (K5, p0[1:2], k1, p0[1:1], k3[1:0]) 3 times, k to end of round.

Round 17: (K5, p0[1:2], k1, p0[1:0], pfb0[0:1], k2[0:0], kfb1[1:0]) 3 times, (k8, kfb) 3 times (60 sts).

Round 18: (K5, p0[1:2], k1, p0[1:2], k4[2:0]) 3 times, k to end of round.

Small size Go to Foot Section

Medium and large sizes
Round 19: (K5, p[1:2], k1, p[1:1], pfb[0:1], k[1:0], kfb[1:0]) 3 times, (k9, kfb) 3 times (66 sts).
Round 20: (K5, p[1:2], k1, p[1:2], k[3:1]) 3 times, k to end of round.
Round 21: (K5, p[1:2], k1, p[1:2], k[2:0], kfb) 3 times, (k10, kfb) 3 times (72 sts).
Round 22: (K5, p[1:2], k1, p[1:2], k[4:2]) 3 times, k to end of round.

Medium size Go to Foot Section

Large size only
Round 23: (K5, p2, k1, p2, k1, kfb) 3 times, (k11, kfb) 3 times (78 sts).
Round 24: (K5, p2, k1, p2, k3) 3 times, k to end of round.
Round 25: (K5, p2, k1, p2, k2, kfb) 3 times, (k12, kfb) 3 times (84 sts).
Round 26: (K5, p2, k1, p2, k4) 3 times, k to end of round.

FOOT
The first 31[37:43] sts are the instep sts, the last 29[35:41] sts are the sole sts. The sole sts are worked in St st.

Work Foot Chart on the instep sts and continue working St st over the sole sts until work measures 4[4³⁄₄:5¹⁄₂]in (10[12:14])cm less than desired finished length, ending with an odd numbered row.

GUSSET
Round 1: Work Foot Chart on instep sts as set, pm, mkfb, k to last st, kfb.
Round 2: Work Foot Chart on instep sts as set, sm, knit to end.
Round 3: Work Foot Chart on instep sts as set, pm, mkfb, k to last st, kfb.
Rep rounds 2 and 3 increasing, 2 sts every alt round until you have 59[71:83] sole sts, ending with round 3.

HEEL
Work Foot Chart on instep sts as set, sm. Make a note of the chart row you have just worked. Heel is now worked flat over the sole sts.
Row 1: K43[52:61] sts, ksw, turn.
Row 2: Sl1, p27[33:39], psw, turn.
Row 3: Sl1, k25[31:37], ksw, turn.
Row 4: Sl1, p23[29:35], psw, turn.
Cont working short rows and shadow wraps as set.
Last row: Sl1, p7[5:7], psw, turn.

Heel flap

Row 1: Sl1, k17[19:23], ssk, turn

Row 2: Sl1, p27[33:39], p2tog, turn.

Row 3: (Sl1, k1) 14[17:20] times, ssk, turn.

Row 4: Sl1, p27[33:39], p2tog, turn.

Row 5: Sl2, (k1, sl1) 13[16:19] times, k1, ssk, turn.

Row 6: Sl1, p27[33:39], p2tog, turn.

Rep rows 3 through 6 until 1 unworked heel st rems on each side.

Return to working in the round.

LEG

Set-up round: (Sl1, k1) 14[17:20] times, ssk. New start of round.

Round 1: Continue working instep as set (note Foot Chart row just worked), sm, k2tog, k to end (60[72:84] sts).

Round 2: Work the next row of Leg Chart to the Pattern Repeat line. New start of round. For example, if you ended with row 8 of Foot Chart in Round 1, work row 9 of Leg Chart as follows: k2 to the pattern repeat line.

New start of round.

Round 3: Work the pattern repeat from the remainder of Leg Chart row to the end of round. For example if you worked row 9 in round 2 above, finish the pattern repeat from row 9.

From this point forward, work only the pattern repeat sts from Leg Chart, ignoring the sts in green squares.

Round 4: Continue working only the pattern repeat section from Leg Chart as set. For example, if you worked row 9 previously, work only the pattern repeat in row 10.

Cont working the pattern repeat section from Leg Chart as set until the leg measures 5in (13cm) from bottom of heel to top of cuff, ending with row 13 of Leg Chart.

CUFF

Round 1: Work row 1 of Cuff Chart.

Round 2: Work row 2 of Cuff Chart.

Cont in this manner until all 8 rows of Cuff Chart have been worked.

Rep row 8 of Cuff Chart until ribbing is 1in (2.5cm) long.

FINISHING

Bind off loosely.

Foot Chart–large

29 28 27 26 25 24 23 22 21 20 19 18 17 16 15 14 13 12 11 10 9 8 7 6 5 4 3 2 1

Foot Chart–medium

25 24 23 22 21 20 19 18 17 16 15 14 13 12 11 10 9 8 7 6 5 4 3 2 1

Foot Chart–small

21 20 19 18 17 16 15 14 13 12 11 10 9 8 7 6 5 4 3 2 1

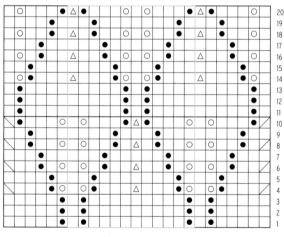

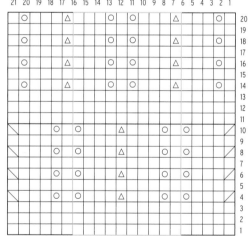

Cuff Chart–large

14 13 12 11 10 9 8 7 6 5 4 3 2 1

Cuff Chart–medium

12 11 10 9 8 7 6 5 4 3 2 1

Cuff Chart–small

10 9 8 7 6 5 4 3 2 1

Leg Chart–large

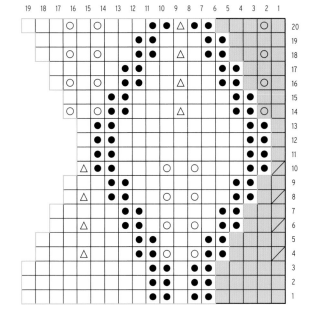

Leg Chart–medium

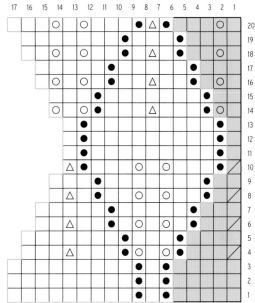

Leg Chart–small

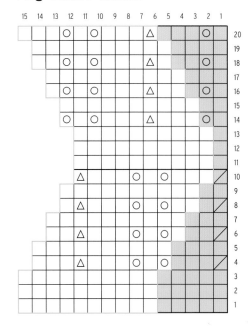

CHART KEY

☐	knit	△	sl1, k2tog, psso
╱	k2tog	╲	ssk
●	purl	○	yo
▨	leg set up only	☐	pattern repeat

De Stijl

These socks use an unusual method to create multilevel
strands, gorgeous in highly variegated yarns as the stranding
helps the color stand out. They're pure form, with simple
lines creating an eye-catching design, and a homage
to the De Stijl art movement.

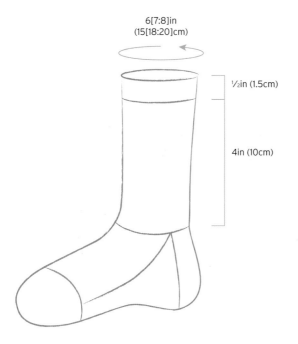

6[7:8]in
(15[18:20]cm)

½in (1.5cm)

4in (10cm)

SOCK VITALS

Yarn

Sokkusu Xtra 70% merino 20% cashmere 10% nylon (400yds/366m per 113g):
1 skein in Corallina

Needles

US 1 (2.25mm) and US 1.5 (2.5mm) or size needed to obtain correct gauge

Gauge

32 sts to 4in (10cm) over stockinette stitch using size 1.5 needles

Notions

Crochet hook for provisional cast on
Stitch markers
Tapestry needle

Pattern notes

When stranding be sure to strand loosely enough to allow the sock to stretch properly, but not so much that the strands look sloppy. You can do this in two ways: either spread the 8 slipped sts out on the needle between the anchoring purl sts so the strand is longer than the width of the stitches; or with the slipped sts sitting flat, wrap the yarn 2 or 3 times around the needle just before the second anchoring purl st, then drop the wraps on the next row. I found that working with the slipped sts uncramped, but unstretched, stranding and wrapping the yarn twice before the second anchoring purl st is just right. Experiment with the first round to find the ideal method to suit your personal knitting style.

CUFF

With a size 1.5 needle and crochet hook, cast on 54[63:72] sts using a crochet provisional cast on; join for knitting in the round, being careful not to twist the sts.
Knit 16 rounds.

Carefully unravel the provisional cast on and slip the held cast-on sts onto smaller needles. Fold hem and hold the needles together so that the cast-on sts are behind the working sts.
Next round: Knit together each working st with a cast-on st until all of the cast-on sts have been worked.

LEG

Note: Because a full round of strands requires 55[64:73] sts, the start of rounds 5 through 8 is moved by one st; the original start of the round is restored in round 9.
Rounds 1-3: Knit.

Stranding

Round 4 (Strand 1): *P1, sl8 wyif, rep from *
5[6:7] times more. **1**

Round 5 (Strand 2): Bring yarn to back, sl1 wyib,
*p1, sl8 wyif, rep from * 5[6:7] times more.

Rounds 6 to 8 (Strands 3, 4 and 5): Rep
round 5. **2**

Round 9: Bring yarn to back, sl1 wyib,
k49[58:67] to restore original end of round.

Rounds 10-13: Knit.

Round 14: *K4, pick up Strand 1 with left needle
from front to back (be sure it is not twisted)
and knit this together with next st, pick up next
strand from front to back (pick it up behind
previous strand) and knit this together with
next st. **3** **4** **5**

Continue picking up strands as set from behind
the previous strand until all 5 strands have
been worked; rep from * 5[6:7] times more.
Rep rounds 1 through 14 five times more.
Knit 3 rounds.

HEEL

The heel is worked flat over the first 27[33:36] sts. The remaining sts are held for the instep.

Set-up row: K27[33:36], turn.
Row 1: (WS) Sl1, p to end, turn.
Row 2: (RS) Sl1, k to end, turn.
Work last 2 rows 13[14:14] times total.

Heel turn

Row 1: (WS) Sl1, p14[17:18], p2tog, p1, turn.
Row 2: (RS) Sl1, k4[4:3], ssk, k1, turn.
Row 3: Sl1, p5[5:4] (one st before gap), p2tog, p1, turn.
Row 4: Sl1, k6[6:5] (one st before gap), ssk, k1, turn.
Cont in this manner until 19[19:20] sts rem. Do not turn.

Small size only

Next row: Sl1, p11, p2tog, p2tog, turn.
Next row: Sl1, k12, ssk, ssk (15 sts). Do not turn.

GUSSET SHAPING

Round 1: Pick up and k14[15:15] sts in the slipped sts down the side of the heel flap, k1 from the held instep sts, pm, k to 1 st from end of instep sts, pm, k1, pick up and k14[15:15] sts up the side of the heel flap, k to end. The sts between the markers are the instep sts. The sts before the first marker and after the second marker are the sole sts (70[79:86] sts).
Round 2: K13[14:14] tbl, k2tog, sm, k to next marker, sm, ssk, k13[14:14] tbl, k to end.
Round 3: Knit.
Round 4: K to within 1 st of marker, k2tog, k to next marker, ssk, k to end.
Rep rounds 3 and 4 until 54[63:72] sts rem.

FOOT

K to within 1 st of marker. This is the new start of round.
Continue knitting in the round, removing any markers, until foot measures ½in (4cm) less than desired finished length.

TOE

Medium size only
Set-up round: K30, *k9, k2tog, rep from * twice more (60 sts).

All sizes
Round 1: *K7[8:10], k2tog, rep from * 5 times more (6 sts decreased, 48[54:66] sts).
Round 2: Knit.
Round 3: *K6[7:9], k2tog, rep from * 5 times more (6 sts decreased, 42[48:60] sts).
Cont to dec 6 sts on every alt round as set until 6 sts rem.

FINISHING

Cut yarn, leaving an 8in (20cm) tail. With tail threaded on a tapestry needle, graft toe shut. Weave in ends.

Fiori di Zucca

My first ever sock club design, which debuted in 2008;
this sock has a special place in my heart. A gentle scalloped
cuff flows into a beautiful eighteenth-century stitch pattern
that reminds me of zucchini flowers. The Cat Bordhi sock
architecture allows for an elegant heel, which melts into
the foot without ruining the lines of the flowers.

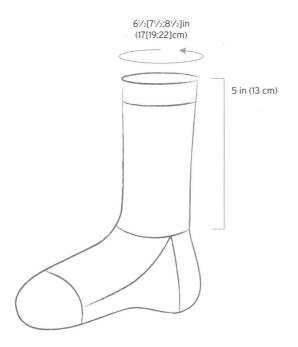

6½[7½:8½]in
(17[19:22]cm)

5 in (13 cm)

SOCK VITALS

Yarn
Sokkusu Lightweight 100% superwash merino
(472yds/432m per 100g):
1 skein in Dengyldene Freden

Needles
Small: US 1 (2.25mm) or size needed to
obtain gauge
Medium and Large: US 1.5 (2.5mm) or size
needed to obtain gauge

Gauge
Small: 42 sts to 4in (10cm) over stockinette stitch
Medium and Large: 36 sts to 4in (10cm) over
stockinette stitch

Notions
Cable needle (cn)
Tapestry needle

Technique notes

ksw (knit shadow wrap): See Kwalla p54.
psw (purl shadow wrap): See Kwalla p56.
LT (left twist): See Farmer McGregor p62.
RT (right twist): See Farmer McGregor
p62.
m1L (make one left): See Mince Pie
Mayhem p112.
m1R (make one right): See Mince Pie
Mayhem p112.
mp (make one purl): Lift bar between
stitches from back to front and purl.

LEG
Note: Doubled-tail long-tail cast on is a
modified long-tail cast on (see page 70).

Cast on 64[64:68] sts using doubled-tail long-
tail cast on. Join to work in the round being
careful not to twist the sts.
The start of round shifts on rounds 29 and 41.
Rounds 1-28: Work rows 1-28 of Leg Chart
(working the chart twice every round).
Round 29: K2[2:1], p1[1:2], work row 29 of Leg
Chart. New start of round.
Rounds 30-39: Work rows 30-39 of Leg Chart.
Round 40: Work Leg Chart to 4[4:5] sts before
the end of round. P1[1:2]. New start
of round.
Rounds 41-52: Work rows 41-52 of Leg Chart.
Repeat rounds 29-40 again.

HEEL
Arch expansion
Note: The arch expansion is worked as increases while knitting in the round.

Rounds 1-11: Work rows 1-11 of Arch Expansion Chart.

Round 12: Work row 12 of Arch Expansion Chart. Note that an extra 3 sts are worked (marked in green on the chart) at the end of the round, shifting the start of the next round by 3 sts.

Rounds 13-24: Work rows 13-24 of Arch Expansion Chart.

Heel cup
Note: The heel cup is worked flat from this point forward.

Row 1: K34[34:35], ksw, turn.

Row 2: Sl1, p30[30:31], psw, turn.

Row 3: Sl1, k to last single st, ksw, turn.

Row 4: Sl1, p to last unwrapped st, psw, turn.
Rep rows 3 and 4 until you have 12 twinned sts on each side and 8[8:10] unwrapped sts between them.

Heel turn
Row 1: Sl1, k to first twinned st, k11, ssk, turn.

Row 2: Sl1, p to first twinned st, p11, p2tog, turn.

Row 3: Sl1, k to one st before gap, ssk (1 st from each side of the gap), turn.

Row 4: Sl1, p to one st before gap, p2tog (1 st from each side of the gap), turn.
Repeat rows 3 and 4 ten more times.

FOOT
Note: From this point forward, return to knitting in the round.

Set-up round: Sl1, k30[30:32], pm for new start of round.

Round 1: Sl2 (1 st from each side of the gap) onto a cable needle and hold at back, k the next st, then k2tog from the cable needle (cn), k5, p1[1:2], yo, k4, ssk, k6, k2tog, k4, yo, p1[1:2], k5, sl 1 onto cn and hold in front, k2tog (1 st from each side of the gap), then k st on cn, pm, k30[30:32] (64[64:68] sts).
The first 34[34:36] sts are the instep sts, the last 30[30:32] stsw are the sole sts which are worked in st st.

Round 2: Work row 2 of Foot Chart to marker, k to end.

Rounds 3 through 24: Cont working corresponding row of Foot Chart and sole sts as set.
Cont working instep sts in patt and sole sts in St st until work measures 2in (5cm) less than desired finished length, ending with row 4, 8, 12, 16, 20 or 24 of Foot Chart.

TOE

Set-up round: RT, k30[30:32], LT, k30[30:32], remove marker, k1, pm for new start of round.
Round 1: K1, ssk, k26[26:28], k2tog, k1, pm, k1, remove old marker, ssk, k26[26:28], k2tog, k1 (60[60:64] sts).

Round 2: Knit.

Round 3: K1, ssk, k to within 3 sts of marker, k2tog, k1, sm, k1, ssk, k to last 3 sts, k2tog, k1 (56[56:60] sts).

Round 4: Knit.

Rep rounds 3 and 4 until 32 sts rem.
Rep round 3 only until 12 sts rem.

FINISHING

Cut yarn, leaving an 8in (20cm) tail. With tail threaded on a tapestry needle, graft toe shut. Weave in ends.

Leg Chart–large

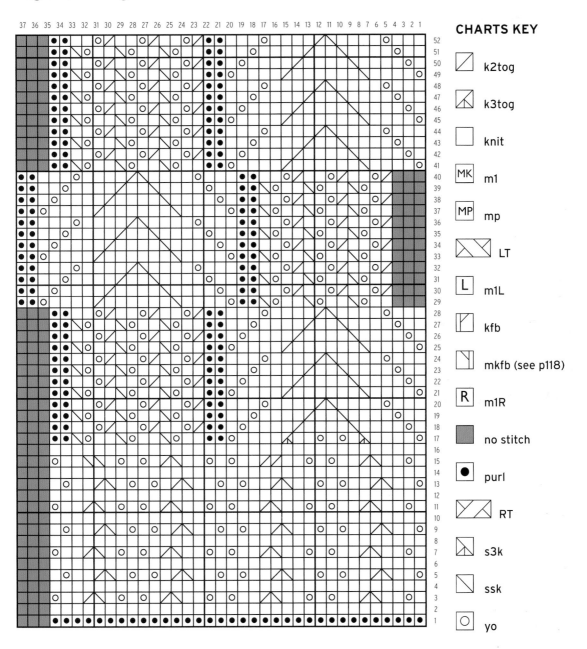

CHARTS KEY

⊘ k2tog	
⊠ k3tog	
□ knit	
MK m1	
MP mp	
⊠ LT	
L m1L	
kfb	
mkfb (see p118)	
R m1R	
no stitch	
● purl	
⊠ RT	
⊠ s3k	
⊠ ssk	
○ yo	

Leg Chart—medium/small

Foot Chart–large

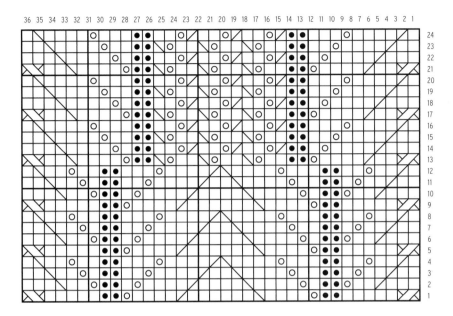

Foot Chart–medium/small

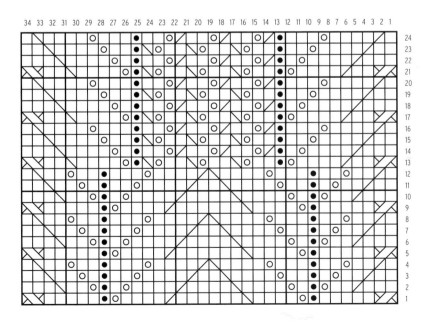

Arch Expansion Chart–large

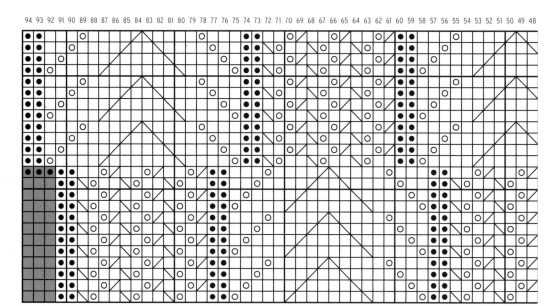

Arch Expansion Chart–medium/small

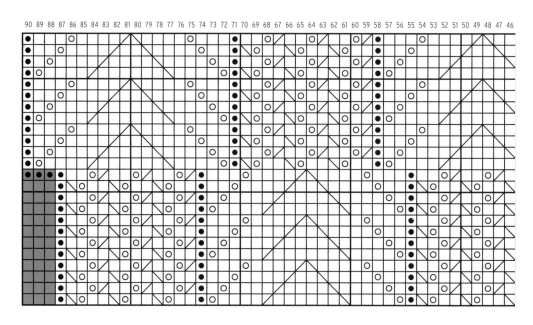

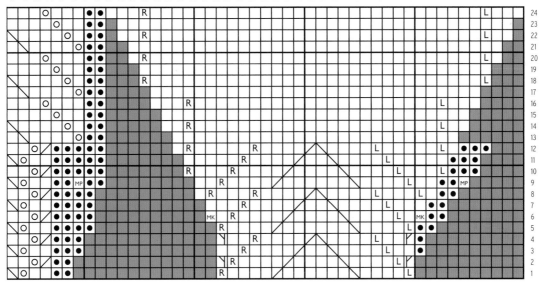

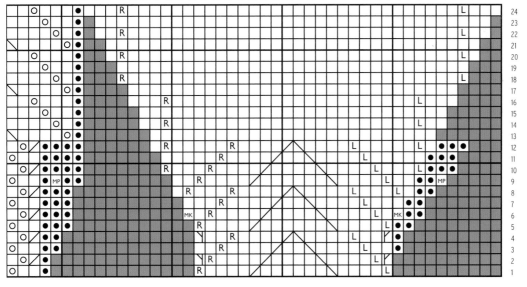

Caretta Caretta

Glamorous and elegant, these shapely socks are beaded
to add an extra sparkle. The stitch pattern with its curves
and points reminded me of tortoise shells and are named
after the endangered loggerhead turtles; the beads hint
at sun glinting of the water droplets on their backs.

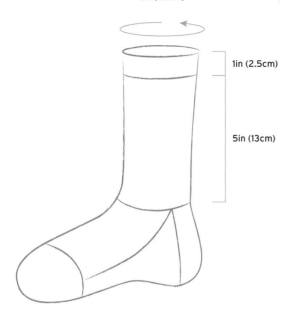

3in (7.5cm)

1in (2.5cm)

5in (13cm)

SOCK VITALS

Yarn
Sokkusu Xtra 70% merino 20% cashmere 10% nylon (400yds/366m per 113g):
1 skein in Fontainebleau

Needles
US 1.5 (2.5mm) or size needed to obtain correct gauge

Gauge
36 sts to 4in (10cm) over stockinette stitch

Notions
360 size 8 seed beads
Big eye beading needle
Tapestry needle

Technique notes

LByo (left bead yarn over): Yo, then slide a bead up next to the stitch. When knitting the yo on the next round, be sure the bead stays on the left of the yo, next to the yo's left st.

RByo (right bead yarn over): Slide a bead up to the needle, yo. When knitting the yo on the next round, be sure the bead stays on the right of the yo, next to the yo's right st.

Pattern notes
Beads must be strung onto the yarn before knitting. If you plan to wear the socks in close-fitting shoes, don't place beads on pressure areas such as above the heel and on the instep. The pattern as written assumes two and one-half repeats each of the Leg Chart and the Foot Chart. For longer socks, you'll need to string more beads. The Leg Chart requires 48 beads over 64 sts for each pattern repeat, and the Foot Chart requires 24 beads over the instep sts for each pattern repeat. It's better to string too many than too few beads so you won't need to cut the yarn to add more. The lace pattern is quite stretchy. You can adjust the sizing by changing the gauge and or adjusting the number of sole sts. For a smaller sock, knit at 36 sts to 4in (10cm).

SET-UP

String 180 beads onto the yarn with a big eye beading needle (this is for one sock only). You may need to thin the yarn slightly by removing 1 or 2 plies where it doubles over itself in the beading needle so it will pass through the beads easily.

CUFF

Cast on 64 sts. Join for knitting in the round being careful not to twist sts.

Round 1: * K3, p1, rep from * to end.
Rep round 1 until rib measures 1in (2.5cm).

LEG

Work rows 1 through 24 of Leg Chart twice, then work rows 1 through 11 once more.

HEEL

The heel is now worked flat and 33 sts are held for the instep.

Row 1: (RS) M1, k3, *p1, k3, rep from * 6 times more, m1, turn (33 heel sts).

Row 2: Sl1, p3, *k1, p3, rep from * to last st, p1, turn.

Row 3: Sl1, k3, *p1, k3, rep from * to last st, k1, turn.

Rep rows 2 and 3 fourteen times more.

Heel turn

Row 1: Sl1, p17, p2tog, p1, turn.

Row 2: Sl1, k4, ssk, k1, turn.

Row 3: Sl1, p5 (to 1 st before gap), p2tog, p1 turn.

Row 4: Sl1, k6 (to 1 st before gap), ssk, k1 turn.

Cont in this manner until 19 sts rem, ending with a RS row. Do not turn.

GUSSET

Round 1: Pick up and k1 st in each of the 16 slipped sts down the side of the heel flap, m1, mark new start of round.

Round 2: Work row 1 of Foot Chart on instep sts, pm, m1, pick up and k1 st in each of the 16 slipped sts up the side of the heel flap, k to end. The sts before the marker are the instep sts; the sts after the marker are the sole sts.

Round 3: Work next row of Foot Chart to marker, sm, ssk, k to last 2 sts, k2tog.

Round 4: Work Foot Chart as set to marker, sm, k to end.

Rep rounds 3 and 4 as set, working Foot Chart over instep sts and dec every alt round until 31 sole sts rem (64 sts).

FOOT

Work Foot Chart over instep sts, and k sole sts until foot measures 2in (5cm) less than desired finished length, ending with row 12 or 24.

TOE

Round 1: P1, *k3, p1, rep from * to marker, sm, k to end.

This round sets up the toe ribbing over the instep sts. When working toe ribbing, work sts so that the line of decrease either side of the instep remains constant; the instep will always start p1, decrease column, and end decrease column, p1.

Round 2: P1, ssk, k1, p1, *k3, p1, rep from * to within 4 sts of marker, k1, k2tog, p1, sm, k to end (31 instep sts, 31 sole sts).

Round 3: Work toe ribbing as set, sm, k to end.

Round 4: P1, ssk, work toe ribbing to within 3 sts of marker, k2tog, p1, sm, k1, ssk, k to last 3 sts, k2tog, k1 (4 sts decreased).

Rep rounds 3 and 4, working toe ribbing over instep sts and dec every alt round as set until 22 sts rem, then rep round 4 only until 10 sts rem.

FINISHING

Cut yarn, leaving an 8in (20cm) tail. With tail threaded on a tapestry needle, graft toe shut. Weave in ends.

Leg Chart

Foot Chart

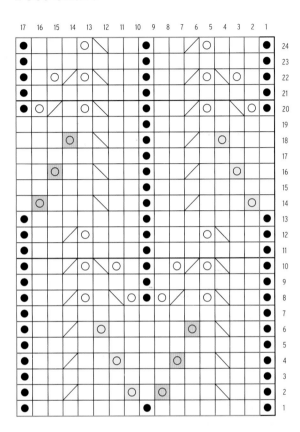

CHART KEY

▣	LByo	◨	ssk
☐	knit	▣	RByo
◪	k2tog	◻	yo
●	purl	☐	pattern repeat

Spring Shoots

Teeny little flower buds poke out from the sock to announce the coming of spring. This is a sock with a twist; using Cat Bordhi's ingenious "afterthought" leg method, the foot is knit as a closed tube, then gasp! horror! cut open to knit the leg. It's really very cathartic once you've gotten over the initial shock. So pour yourself a glass of Dutch courage, steady your hands and ready the scissors. Ready, steady, snip!

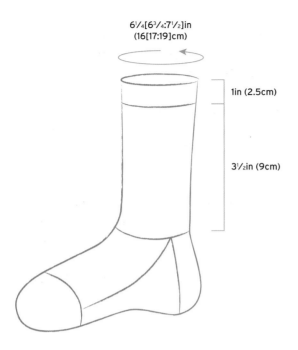

6¼[6¾:7½]in
(16[17:19]cm)

1in (2.5cm)

3½in (9cm)

SOCK VITALS

Yarn

Sokkusu-Original, 100% extra fine superwash merino wool (433yds/396m per 120g):
1 skein in Shepherd's Delight

Needles

US 1.5 (2.5mm) or size needed to obtain correct gauge and one or two sizes smaller set of needles to pick up stitches for afterthought heel

Gauge

36 sts to 4in (10cm) over stockinette stitch on larger needles
34½ sts to 4in (10cm) over bud pattern on larger needles

Notions

Crochet hook for provisional cast on
Stitch markers
Tapestry needle
Waste yarn

Pattern notes

The cast on is a Turkish cast on with a twist (see Hundred Acre Wood, page 118). After the first half of the cast-on sts are knit, in the next round the 6 sts are knit using the tail and working yarn held together as a double strand, giving you a quick rounded increase that remains nice and smooth against your toes. The foot is knit as a closed tube, and then (deep breath!) snipped open to accommodate an "afterthought" leg.

When you knit the bud pattern on the leg, the second slipped st of the last ssk in round 12 is actually the first st of the next round; the second "petal" of the last bud of the round is wrapped around the first st of the next round. Ignore the st count for the next round; simply keep the start of round in the usual place.

TOE

Use the Turkish cast-on method as shown on page 118. Leave a 5in (13cm) tail and bring yarn over two needles held together with points to the right. Wrap the working yarn around both needles 3 times, working from left to right and swinging the yarn away from you and then back toward you over the top of both needles.

Set-up round: Using bottom needle if using circulars, or third needle if using DPNs, k3 from the top needle.

Round 1: Holding tail and working yarn together as a double strand, k6 (12 sts).

Round 2: K12, being careful to knit each of the double strand sts (12 sts).

Round 3: *K1, kfb, rep from * to end (6 sts increased–18 sts).

Round 4: Knit.

Round 5: *K2, kfb, rep from * to end (24 sts). Rep inc rounds as set, inc 6 sts on every alt round until there are 54[60:66] sts. Cont knitting every round until work reaches bottom of pinky toenail when you try it on.

FOOT

The first 27[31:31] sts are the instep sts. The rem 27[29:35] sts are the sole sts. The sole sts are worked in st st. After the first 14 rounds, the sole sts will increase by 2 sts every 4th round until a total of 18 sts are increased.

Begin Bud Pattern

Round 1: K3, *(k1, yo, k1, in the next st, wrapping the yarn over the needle twice for each of the knit sts), k3, rep from * 5[6:6] times more, k the sole sts.

Round 2: K3, *sl3 wyib (dropping the extra wraps), k3, rep from * 5[6:6] times more, k the sole sts.

Rounds 3 and 4: Rep round 2.

Round 5: K2, *k2tog, k1, ssk, k1, rep from * 5[6:6] times more, k1, k the sole sts.

Rounds 6 and 7: Knit.

Round 8: K5, *(k1, yo, k1, in the next st, wrapping the yarn over the needle twice for each of the knit sts), k3, rep from * 4[5:5] times more, k2, k the sole sts.

Round 9: K5, *sl3 wyib (dropping the extra wraps), k3, rep from * 4[5:5] times more, k2, k the sole sts.

Rounds 10 and 11: Rep round 9.

Round 12: K4, *k2tog, k1, ssk, k1, rep from * 4[5:5] times more, k3, k the sole sts.

Rounds 13 and 14: Knit.

Cont working rounds 1 through 14 and at the same time inc 2 sts evenly on every 4th round on the sole sts until there are 45[47:53] sole sts.

Cont until work measures the span of your hand from the tip of your longest finger to the wrist line. This corresponds for most people to the length of the foot from the tip of the toes to the midline of the ankle. End with round 6 or 13. Thread a safety line through the 27[31:31] instep sts.

HEEL

Knit 2 rounds. Thread another safety line through the 27[31:31] instep sts. Cont knitting every round until the work measures 1½in (4cm) less than desired finished length. Work heel decreases as follows:

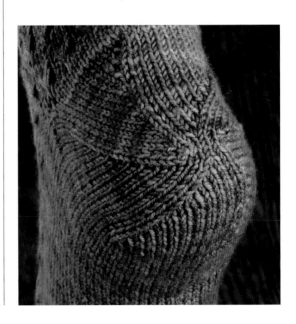

Round 1: *K10[11:12], k2tog, rep from * to end.
Round 2: Knit.
Round 3: *K9[10:11], k2tog, rep from * to end.
Round 4: Knit.
Cont to dec 6 sts on every alt round until 12 sts rem. Cut the working yarn, leaving an 8in (20cm) tail. Thread rem sts onto waste yarn.

LEG
(see Technique notes and images on opposite page)
The sts on the safety lines will be transferred to the smaller needles, adjusting for extra sts for the leg. Be sure to leave one row of sts between the two safety lines, as this middle row is the one that gets snipped. The instructions assume you work clockwise (as you would knit in the round).
Using the smaller needles, pm for start of round.

Small and medium sizes only
Place 27[31] held instep sts on the first safety line onto the smaller needle.
Pick up the next st at the end of the first safety line and place it onto the needle.
Pick up the first st before the start of the second safety line and place it onto the needle.
Place 27[31] sts held on the second safety line onto a second needle (56[64] sts).

Large size only
Pick up the 2 sts before the start of the first safety line and place them onto the needle.
Place 31 sts held instep sts on the first safety line onto the needle.
Pick up the next 3 sts at the end of the first safety line and place them onto the needle.
Pick up the 3 sts before the start of the second

Technique note

Snipping
The photos show 2 sts being picked up either side the lifelines; the number of sts to pick up will vary depending on the size of sock being knit.
Sample with life lines. **1**
Pick up two stitches before the start of a lifeline. **2**
Pick up the stitches on the lifeline. **3**
Turn sample sock around after picking up two more stitches at the end of the lifeline, and do the same again for the second lifeline. **4**
Snip the yarn in the row between the lifelines. **5**
Unravel middle row to last two stitches either side, leaving these in situ. **6**

safety line and place them onto the needle.
Place 31 sts held on the second safety line onto the needle.
Pick up the next 2 sts at the end of the second safety line and place them onto the needle (72 sts).

All sizes
Carefully cut only the middle row between the two rows of sts now on the needles. Unravel the cut yarn to within 2 sts of each needle end (8 sts will have the cut yarn still woven in: 4 on the left side of the opening and 4 on the right side of the opening, 2 up 2 down). The cut yarn rem in the corner sts keeps the stress points strong and helps prevent gaps.
From the start of round marker, remove marker,

Snipping

count back 16[16:14] sts and pm for new start of round at the back of the leg. Attach the working yarn and switch to the larger needles.

Knit one round.

If the last patt round on your foot was Round 6, start with round 1 below. If your last patt round on your foot was Round 13, start with round 8 below.

Round 1: K1, *(k1, yo, k1, in next st, wrapping the yarn over the needle twice for each of the knit sts), k3, rep from * 12[14:16] times more, (k1, yo, k1, in next st, wrapping the yarn over the needle twice for each of the knit sts), k2.

Round 2: K1, *sl3 wyib (dropping the extra wraps), k3, rep from * 12[14:16] times more, sl 3 wyib, k2.

Rounds 3 and 4: Rep round 2.

Round 5: *K2tog, k1, ssk, k1, rep from * 13[15:17] times more.

Rounds 6 and 7: Knit.

Round 8: *K3, (k1, yo, k1, in next st, wrapping the yarn over the needle twice for each of the

knit sts), rep from * 13[15:17] times more.

Round 9: *K3, sl3 wyib (dropping the extra wraps), rep from * 13[15:17] times more.

Rounds 10 and 11: Rep round 9.

Round 12: K2, *k2tog, k1, ssk, k1, rep from * 12[14:16] times more, k2tog, k1, ssk.

Note that the second slipped st of the last ssk in the round is actually the first st of round 13. Ignore the st count in round 13 and keep the start of the round in the same place.

Rounds 13 and 14: Knit.

Continue working rounds 1 through 14 until leg measures 6in (15cm) from heel, ending with round 7 or 14.

CUFF

Crochet a provisional cast on of 7 sts using waste yarn onto the left needle.

Set-up row: With RS facing, k 7 sts. The provisional cast on should now be sitting under 7 sts on the right needle. These 7 sts form the cuff, which is worked flat in seed st and attached to the live sts on the leg every WS row by purling together the last st of the cuff band with a live st from the leg.

Row 1: (WS) (K1, p1) 3 times, p2tog.

Row 2: (RS) Sl1, (p1, k1) 3 times.

Rep rows 1 and 2 until all leg sts have been worked, ending with a WS row.

Cut yarn, leaving a 7in (18cm) tail. Pull the tail through the last st.

Using a tapestry needle, thread the tail through the first slipped st of the cuff edge, then back through the last p2tog st to close the gap (6 sts).

FINISHING

Remove provisional cast on from the cuff and place 6 sts onto a second needle. Graft the cuff band edges together. Place held heel sts on needles and graft closed. Weave ends in. Block if desired.

General Information

Working from charts Always begin knitting charts from the bottom and work upwards. When working in the round, work all chart rows from right to left. When working flat, you should work right-side rows from right to left and wrong-side rows from left to right. Note too that on wrong-side rows the chart symbols change, i.e. a knit stitch on the right side is worked as a purl stitch on the wrong side.

Diagrams The little sock diagram on each pattern represents the finished measurements of the sock, blocked but unstretched.

DPNs and circulars The patterns in this book are written generically for both DPNs and circulars. With DPNs divide the stitches between the needles as you wish–it may help to have a stitch marker to mark the beginning of the round and the separation between instep sts and sole sts, or to place the instep sts on separate needles to the sole sts.

Slipping stitches Slipped sts should always be slipped purlwise with yarn in back on the RS, and with yarn in front on the WS, unless specified otherwise.

Standard Abbreviations

cm	centimeter
in	inch
k	knit
k2tog	knit 2 sts together
k3tog	knit 3 sts together
k4tog	knit 4 sts together
kfb	knit forward back
m1	make 1 by lifting bar between sts from front to back and knitting tbl
p	purl
pfb	purl forward back. Purl into the next stitch normally. Taking the left needle, insert from back to front in stitch below the stitch just made (i.e. the loop that had been on the left needle), and purl into it again
p2tog	purl 2 sts together
pm	place marker
psso	pass slipped stitch over
rem	remain(ing)
rep	repeat

RS	right side
s3k	slip 3 knitwise, 1 at a time, k3tog tbl
s4k	slip 4 knitwise, 1 at a time, k4tog tbl
sl	slip
sm	slip marker
ssk	slip 2 sts knitwise one at a time, pass the two slipped sts back to left needle, knit both together through the back loop
ssp	slip 2 knitwise one at a time, pass two slipped sts back to left needle, purl two slipped sts together from the back, left to right.
st(s)	stitch(es)
St st	stockinette stitch
tbl	through back loop
tog	together
WS	wrong side
wyib	with yarn in back
wyif	with yarn in front
WT	wrap and turn
yo	yarn over

Resources

I'm a book learner. Montse Stanley's *The Knitters Handbook* has been an inspiration and my favorite teacher. There are plenty of videos and pictorial tutorials online to help clarify techniques which may not be familiar. Explore and learn my Jedi knitters, for the knitting force is strong in you.

ONLINE HELP

Knitters Review

www.knittersreview.com

Impartial review of yarns, tools, and books by Clara Parkes. Her free weekly newsletter is filled with all manner of information: yarn and tool reviews, event listings, and Clara's gentle but cheeky humour.

Knitty

www.knitty.com

A free online magazine edited by Amy Singer. Informative articles on techniques as well as a huge archive of lovely sock patterns.

Ravelry

www.ravelry.com

The forums on Ravelry are a great place to find answers to just about any knitting question you may have. The database of patterns and designers is a treasure trove of inspiration. Join the Socktopod's group and connect with like-minded sock knitters.

TUTORIALS

YouTube is home to an abundance of video tutorials for all manner of knitting techniques. Cat Bordhi has YouTube videos for the Turkish cast on and for snipping an "afterthought" leg. You can find links to Cat's videos here: *(http://www.catbordhi.com/pf.html)*. For basic techniques such as grafting try *www.knittinghelp.com*.

BOOKS/DVDS

For techniques, my go-to reference book is Montse Stanley's excellent *Knitters Handbook*, published by Reader's Digest Association.

Clara Parkes's books *The Knitter's Book of Yarn*, *The Knitter's Book of Wool*, and *The Knitters Book of Socks*, all published by Random House, are wonderfully informative.

Cat Bordhi continues to thrill with her innovative approach to socks. *New Pathways for Sock Knitters* and *Personal Footprints for Insouciant Sock Knitters* (Passing Paws Press) are both must-reads for any sock knitter who wants to explore alternative ways of creating socks. *Personal Footprints for Insouciant Sock Knitters* also has details on tailoring an "afterthought" leg sock for perfect fit.

For pure sock beauty and inspiration, do check out *Cookie A's Sock Innovation* (Interweave Press) and her eye candy follow up *knit. sock. love.* (One Leg Press).

Lucy Neatby's DVD series, *Learn with Lucy: DVDs for all knitters*, which can be found at *www.lucyneatby.com*, (and classes if you are lucky enough take one) contain a wealth of information to help take your knitting skills to the next level.

Nola Fournier and Jane Fournier's *In Sheep's Clothing: A Handspinner's Guide to Wool* is a good source of information on fiber. Published by Interweave Press Inc.

Yarns

The socks in this book are all knit with Socktopus Sokkusu sock yarns. There are, however, many indie dyers out there who produce amazing yarns suitable for knitting socks; part of the thrill of knitting your own socks is discovering new yarns yourself. Here are a few to get you started:

Socktopus Yarns and Designs
www.socktopus.co.uk

Shelridge Farm
www.shelridge.com

Old Maiden Aunt
www.oldmaidenaunt.com

Natural Dye Studio
www.thenaturaldyestudio.com

Lorna's Laces
www.lornaslaces.net

Koigu Wool Designs
www.koigu.com

Hazel Knits
www.hazelknits.com

Fyberspates
www.fyberspates.co.uk

Easyknits
www.easyknits.co.uk

Dream in Color
www.dreamincoloryarn.com

Blue Moon Fiber Arts
www.bluemoonfiberarts.com

Rohrspatz & Wollmeise
www.rohrspatzundwollmeise.de

Special thanks to John Arbon Textiles (jarbon.com) for generously providing the fibre samples on p15, Jeni Brown of Fyberspates for providing Sheila Gold Sparkle Sock and Jon Dunn of Easyknits for providing Bamboo Merino sock, both for the swatches section.

Acknowledgments

Six short years ago I knit my very first sock. A couple of years later I launched Socktopus, quit my job as a City lawyer, designed my first sock pattern; I haven't look back since. I owe a huge debt of gratitude to all the knitters out there–the men and women who keep the craft alive, the innovators whose minds puzzle out the secrets of new techniques, tips and tricks, the designers whose beautiful creations keep my knitting mojo buzzing, all my Socktopods for their support, love and {{hugs}} over the years. Without these lovely people, in whose number I include you, dear reader, I could never have known the life-changing utter pleasure of burying my face in a pile of handpainted cashmere, or have anyone with whom to share such yarnie delights.

This book would not be, if not for Jonathan Bailey who immediately got the beauty of hand-knit socks and gave me the opportunity to write it. Judith Chamberlain-Webber, my UK editor, deserves a Melchizedek of wine not only for her deft editing and skilful shepherding through the book writing process, but also for her unfailing ability to manage my stressy-itis fits with calm and grace. A very large, and very heartfelt, thank you.

Two others worked hand-in-hand with Judith and I-Judith Durant my US editor turned my Canadian/British text into US English for Taunton and Anni Howard tech-edited every pattern and saved the day with her clean and lovely charts. A whole team of sample knitters gave form to my creations, and another team of test knitters helped to make the patterns as error free as possible. To each and everyone: I couldn't have done it without you. Thank you from the bottom of my heart.

I would also like to thank Jane McGuinness for her whimsical and gorgeous illustrations on pages 16–19, Aimee Gille for providing the photo of her Paris yarn shop cum tea room L'Oisivethe on page 13 and Lizzy House for my Sock Club owl on page 3. A special thanks goes to Cookie A for her insight and seasoned counsel.

And finally: Thanks mom and dad for always believing in me, and giving me the confidence and the determination to master anything I set my mind to. David, you have my love and everlasting gratitude for taking my knitting life in stride and for never ever questioning my stash.

Sample (in bold) and test knitters:

TOTALLY VANILLA:
Neiline Michael
Yvonne Moore

KANDAHAR:
Harriet Fears Davies
Neiline Michael
Danièle Rousseau
Marja Lindstrom

V JUNKIE:
Caroline Wright
Simone Dräger
Sarah Johnson

KWALLA:
Judith Daykin
Helen Kurtz
Agnieszka Kazmierczak

FARMER McGREGOR:
Yuvinia Yuhadi
Karen Bowen

SHUR'TUGAL:
Alisha Irish
Angie Kachelmeier
Laura Shirley

2LUVCREW:
Ai-Ling Lee
Constance Cole
Nicole Salzmann

VORTICITY:
Dee Desai-Tagg
Susan Dick

RUMPLED!:
Patricia Hill
Cheryl Read
Gill Hills

CROWLEY:
Michaela Moores
Maire Martin
Ute Kahle

OM SHANTI:
Kate Woolly
Simone Dräger
Angelina Paolitto

MINCE PIE MAYHEM:
Michaela Moores
Melissa Gillispie
Deborah Terrio

HUNDRED ACRE WOOD:
Patricia Hill
Elizabeth Hamanishi
Jememah A. Baker

DE STIJL:
Rachel Atkinson
Lynn Hensley
Silke Pieper

FIORI DI ZUCCA:
Susan Dick
Nancy Reinstein
Sabine Naumann

CARETTA CARETTA:
Mel Howes
Mary Hough
Emily Chu

SPRING SHOOTS:
Nora Brodian
Daisy Blinn
Amanda Bell

Special thanks also to Linda Troeberg.

GMC Publications would like to thank:

Chris Gloag and his assistant Guillaume Serve for photography.

Amy from Zone Models.

Jen Dodson for hair and make-up.

Rebecca Mothersole for styling assistance.

Gunn's Florist in Sydney Street, Brighton and Across the Tracks in Gloucester Road, Brighton, for letting us shoot on their premises.

Picture credits:

Owl artwork on spine and page 3: Lizzy House

Artwork on pages 16–19: Jane McGuinness

Page 13: Aimée Gille

Page 14: Flickr.com/shallowend

Studio photography: Anthony Bailey/GMC and Gilda Pacitti/GMC.

Index

Names of projects are printed in bold.